The short guide to community development

Second edition

Alison Gilchrist and Marilyn Taylor

First edition published in 2011
Second edition published in Great Britain in 2016 by

Policy Press
University of Bristol
1-9 Old Park Hill
Bristol BS2 8BB
UK
+44 (0)117 954 5940
pp-info@bristol.ac.uk
www.policypress.co.uk

North America office:
Policy Press
c/o The University of Chicago Press
1427 East 60th Street
Chicago, IL 60637, USA
t: +1 773 702 7700
f: +1 773-702-9756
sales@press.uchicago.edu
www.press.uchicago.edu

British Library Cataloguing in Publication Data
A catalogue record for this book is available from the British Library.

Library of Congress Cataloging-in-Publication Data
A catalog record for this book has been requested.

ISBN 978-1-4473-2783-7 paperback
ISBN 978-1-4473-2784-4 ePub
ISBN 978-1-4473-2785-1 Mobi

Cover design by Policy Press
Front cover image kindly supplied by www.alamy.com
Printed and bound in Great Britain by CMP, Poole
Policy Press uses environmentally responsible print partners

Contents

List of tables and boxes

Table

Boxes

1

introduction

'Community' is a concept that seems always to be in fashion with policy makers – community development, less so. In some quarters, the existence of community is seen as a natural and enduring facet of society; others lament its decline. One of the primary purposes of community development is to boost the effectiveness of community action, participation and capacity. Not everyone sees the necessity of strategic interventions to achieve this. Indeed, the term itself is problematic, with the approach also being called social development, popular education, critical pedagogy, community organising, community engagement and community education, for example. In the UK some writers prefer the term 'critical community practice' (Butcher et al, 2007), which describes a broader approach to working with communities. Nonetheless, internationally, community development is commonly adopted by non-governmental organisations as a means of developing infrastructure, local economic initiatives and democracy. Governments worldwide have introduced community development programmes to tackle poverty and other seemingly intractable social problems. They have also been confronted by communities who have decided to mobilise for themselves, organising services, protest actions and self-help movements to improve living standards and gain important civil rights.

In the 1950s the United Nations defined community development as 'a process designed to create conditions of economic and social progress for the whole community with its active participation' (United Nations, 1955, p 6).

The International Association for Community Development (IACD) recently adopted the following guiding principles for working with communities.

Box 1.1 IACD's understanding of community development

Community development is a set of practices and methods that focus on harnessing the innate abilities and potential that exist in all human communities to become active agents in their own development, and to organise themselves to address key issues and concerns that they share.

Community development workers may be members of the community, paid workers or volunteers. They work with and alongside people in the community to identify concerns and opportunities, and develop the confidence and energy to respond together.

The building of community and social capital is both a core part of the process and an outcome, and in this way there is an extension of co-operative attitudes and practices that are built through community development that can increase community resilience over time.

Source: IACD (2015a)

In the UK the fortunes and status of community development have waxed and waned. As an external intervention, it was initially used by philanthropic bodies (for example, the university settlements) to bring adult education and capacity building to disadvantaged neighbourhoods, such as the London Docklands. Local authorities and housing trusts later employed officers in new towns and estates to encourage residents to set up groups and associations for various leisure and civic purposes in order to generate 'community spirit' and promote self-help.

For a long time, community development raised for policy makers the spectre of the Community Development Projects of the 1970s (Loney, 1983), a government-sponsored programme whose Marxist critique of capitalism – despite striking a chord with many practitioners – was not quite what the programme's sponsors had in mind. Since that time community development has been used to build 'community capacity' and 'social capital', as well as to support 'community empowerment' and participation underpinning new approaches to persistent local problems.

Community development is not a phrase that necessarily travels well. A recent mapping study by the IACD (2015b) found a plethora of terms in use that seemed to cover the core understanding, and noted significant differences in practice between countries on different continents. In the global South community development retains its colonial associations, often devoid of the political content that characterises popular education movements there, for example, in Latin America (Pearce et al, 2010). However, the term maintains its currency. In the US, where 'community development organizations are increasingly assuming the roles of local government' (DeFilippis and Saegert, 2012, p 1), the term describes a mainstream set of practices and institutions. It also continues to have salience in a number of Organisation for Economic Co-operation and Development (OECD) countries, such as Australia and Canada.

There are, of course, many debates about the terminology of community and community development, and we will visit these in the chapters that follow, as well as beginning to unpack some of the terms used above.

A quick review of definitions developed over the years by scholars, practitioners and institutions concerned with community development yields a number of common themes around social change, social justice, collective action, equality and mutual respect, enabling participation, and changing power relationships. One US text echoes the analysis of the Community Development Projects in the UK, arguing that: 'Community development occurs when the conditions of surviving and thriving in a place are not being supplied by capital.' This highlights the need to connect geographical communities to the 'far greater resources, opportunities and power that lie outside [them]' (DeFilippis and Saegert, 2012, p 6). Descriptions from elsewhere in the world emphasise the need to develop political awareness alongside skills, confidence and resources, drawing on the popular education movement in Latin America and the seminal writings of Paulo Freire.

Many definitions acknowledge the need to work with the assets, strengths, knowledge and experience that communities already have, rather than working with the deficit model that policy makers tend to assume. There is, however, some debate over whether community development is an approach, an occupation or a movement. Is it a profession of specialist workers or does it simply indicate a particular way of working in or with communities? Is it about the creation of resources, capacity, infrastructure and leadership for communities to use in whichever ways they choose? Or is it a set of techniques that can be used to accomplish externally defined objectives? Is it a movement for social change? Or maybe community development is simply about the development of 'community' itself? By this we mean not the slippery and abstract concept that has vexed sociologists but the sense of belonging and collective efficacy that people sometimes experience as receiving security, practical help and emotional support from those around them – not only friends and neighbours but also more casual acquaintances drawn from everyday interactions and activities. As we shall examine more closely in Chapter Four, for some people, a sense of community supplies both the focus and the motivation to take action and press for change. The function that community plays in people's lives and in policy will be a theme that we return to throughout the book, examining how community development skills and support are understood and applied by activists, professionals, policy makers and philanthropists to tackle the social, economic and political challenges that face so many post-industrial societies. Box 1.2 below is based on discussions among UK practitioners, members of the now defunct Community Development Exchange.

Box 1.2 What is community development?

Community development can be both an occupation (such as a community development worker in a local authority) and a way of working with communities. Its key purpose is to build communities based on *justice, equality* and *mutual respect*.

Community development involves changing the relationships between ordinary people and people in positions of power, so that everyone can take part in the issues that affect their lives. It starts from the principle that within any community there is a wealth of knowledge and experience which, if used in creative ways, can be channelled into collective action to achieve the community's desired goals.

Community development practitioners work alongside people in communities to help build relationships with key people and organisations and to identify common concerns. They create opportunities for the community to learn new skills and, by enabling people to act together, community development practitioners help to foster social inclusion and equality.

Source: Community Development Exchange (CDX) (2008)

This Short Guide starts in Chapter Two by reviewing definitions and understandings of community development, describing different models and how they differ from related approaches and concepts. The next two chapters look at context and theory. Chapter Three lays out the policies and other factors that have shaped community development over the years, and the policy themes that it is expected to address. In Chapter Four we review some of the theories that can help inform community development practice, focusing particularly on theories of community, psychology, the state, collective organisation and power. Chapters Five and Six come back to the practice of community development. Chapter Five considers the skills, values and techniques that constitute community development practice, how to do it and the infrastructure that is needed to support it. Chapter Six describes how it can be applied in different policy fields. The final two chapters explore the challenges that face community development. Chapter Seven looks at the issues and dilemmas that are inherent within the practice and politics of community development, while Chapter Eight looks at the way external trends are likely to affect its future prospects.

The Guide is written from a UK perspective. However, we have referred to experience and debates elsewhere in the world, particularly in the US, and we believe that many of the issues raised have a wider significance. We end by welcoming the increasing willingness of community development workers in the global North – and policy makers too – to learn from practice in the global South.

This last comment raises some more language issues. Most of the terminology that distinguishes between different regions of the world is problematic: how do we describe the distinction that used to be made between the developed and developing worlds? With apologies to Australasia, we have chosen to use the terms global South and global North.

Finally, while we are on the subject of terminology, we need to outline how we are using the term 'community'. We know that communities are multifaceted and often fragmented, so to talk of 'community' or even 'communities' implies a homogeneity that cannot be assumed. However, in the absence of a clearer term, we have decided to refer to the people that community development works with as communities or community members.

Our intention with this Short Guide is to demonstrate not only the versatility and value of community development to modern society, but also to examine the many ways in which it is contested and challenged by political critiques and practical circumstances. Our broad conclusion is that community development has a great deal to offer communities and professionals working across a whole range of policy goals. For it to be effective and sustainable, however, it needs a strategic investment in the skills, resources and infrastructure that are essential if communities are to play their part in building a more equitable and democratic society.

Further reading

Two comprehensive guides to community development have been updated in recent years. These are Keith Popple's *Analysing community work* (2015) and Alan Twelvetrees' *Community work* (forthcoming) and readers will find much of interest in them. Also recommended are *Critical community practice*, by Butcher et al (2007) and Margaret Ledwith's 2011 book, *Community development: A critical approach.*

For a comprehensive overview of the evolution of community development over time, both in practice and in theory, readers can go to three excellent readers published over the last few years. An international perspective is provided by Gary Craig, Keith Popple and Mae Shaw in *Community development in theory and practice* (2008), which brings together a collection of articles from the international *Community Development Journal* since its inception in 1965. A US perspective is provided by James DeFilippis and Susan Saegert in their *Community development reader* (2nd edn, 2012). Gary Craig and co-editors have also produced a UK collection, *The community development reader: History, themes and issues* (2011), drawing together influential articles and book extracts from a variety of sources from the 1950s to the present day.

Finally, two journals provide a valuable source: *Community Development Journal* and *Community Development*, the journal of the US-based Community Development Society. The CDJ Plus website (www. oxfordjournals.org/cdjc/) carries further publications which can be downloaded free of charge. Readers will also find valuable material in development studies journals, *Development Studies* itself and the *IDS Bulletin*, published by the Institute of Development Studies. *Concept: The Journal of Contemporary Community Education Practice Theory* is another useful source. It is now published online, but a collection of key articles from its first 16 years has been published by Mae Shaw,

Jane Meagher and Stuart Moir in *Participation in community development: Problems and possibilities* (2006).

In addition to these publications, several websites carry useful resources such as guides, reports and policy statements relevant to community development or the issues facing communities. These are listed in the Appendix.

Government programmes often have associated websites so it is worth visiting the relevant government departments or national organisations that host these. Here are a few examples, including websites for Wales, Scotland and Northern Ireland:

www.justact.org.uk/

http://mycommunity.org.uk/

www.communityscot.org.uk/

http://gov.wales/topics/people-and-communities/

https://www.dsdni.gov.uk/

These sites often signpost to current or recent consultations so they are a good way of staying abreast of political and policy developments in the different jurisdictions.

2

what is community development?

This chapter focuses on different understandings of community development. It sets out the core principles and processes that characterise community development and distinguish it from related approaches and concepts. We review different models for working with communities, as well as exploring the relationship between community development and similar approaches to achieving change.

Underpinning principles and processes

As we saw in Chapter One, community development represents a broad approach to working with people in communities to achieve greater levels of social justice. In the main, the focus is on individuals, groups and networks that want or need to co-operate in order to realise change at a local or community level. That change might be driven by an external threat to people's quality of life (for example, the building of new housing on much-loved green space) or it could be shaped by residents' desire to improve services for a particular section of the community (for example, providing facilities for young people to divert them from drugs or vandalism). Adopting a community development approach means ensuring that the issues and priorities are identified and agreed by the communities themselves, and that people are encouraged to work together towards a collective solution to a shared concern.

Community development rests on three vital pillars or processes:

- informal education
- collective action
- organisation development.

Informal education describes the learning that takes place mainly through involvement in community activities, and so it is sometimes described as experiential. People learn new skills through taking on tasks, observing others, 'having a go' and receiving feedback. Opportunities for discussion ensure that useful knowledge and understanding is shared through listening, careful explanation and critical debate. Information and ideas can also be gleaned from relevant materials and official publications as well as informal conversations. Having assumptions challenged through dialogue and testing questions can result in people gaining new understanding and insights that provide alternative perspectives to what may have been learnt at school, or picked up from the media or peers. Informal learning increases people's confidence, their openness to new thinking and their ability to take on unfamiliar roles and responsibilities. It is also about learning to question received wisdom and to challenge authority. For many people, participation in community development activities represents an important step on the journey to active citizenship, a career goal or a sense of self-worth.

Box 2.1 Jatinder's journey

Jatinder joins a playgroup being run at the church hall so that her toddler can learn to socialise. After a few months of regular attendance, she joins the committee and at the annual meeting is persuaded to take on the role of treasurer. She is initially reluctant as she was not good with figures at school, but the community worker persuades her by talking through the role and explaining how to set up a simple accounting system to keep track of the money coming in (mainly from membership fees and the occasional small grant) and the spending. Despite her earlier reservations, Jatinder finds that she is able to do this task easily and that she actually enjoys working with numbers so that, with a little help from the community worker, she is able to prepare the annual accounts. She agrees to represent the group on the local under-fives forum and is invited to go on a course to learn computer-based bookkeeping. She enjoys this so much that she takes responsibility for running the family business accounts and later gets a job as ledger clerk for a small firm. They are so impressed by her enthusiasm and ability that after a couple of years they agree to pay her fees and give her study leave to undertake her accountancy qualifications. Now that her children are at school, she has taken the plunge and runs her own successful accounting business, specialising in support for community groups.

Most of us need feedback and encouragement from others, especially our peers. Community development workers actively support informal education by getting people to think about their experiences, try out new skills, question assumptions and explore new ways of seeing the world.

A central theme of community development is that it supports people to take **collective action** to tackle problems that many individuals may be experiencing or to achieve a shared goal that will have wider benefit. Community development works with people to identify the aims they have in common and supports them to accomplish these. A first step usually involves residents or community members recognising that the difficulties they are facing in their own lives are also being encountered by others. By coming together (sometimes with some kind of community development support), people realise that their combined efforts and talents can change the situation or at least improve their conditions and open up opportunities. This does not necessarily require setting up a formal organisation. The important point is that people are not left to fend for themselves in making complaints or putting forward suggestions as isolated residents. Community development often provides the impetus to mobilise community members to develop a joint plan of action, recruit allies and activists, and decide what needs to be done to make the changes they want. It is about channelling the power of combined voices and determination: the strength of many people acting for their mutual benefit or to champion the interests of those who cannot stand up for themselves.

As individuals develop their capacity, they sometimes need to **develop an organisation** in order to meet the changing demands of members and the expectations of other stakeholders, such as funders. In community development, this means helping a group to find a form that matches its current aims and functions. The structure and procedures should enable members to achieve their goals, to act legally and to be accountable to the membership and wider community, but do not need to be overly formalised. Organisation development may occur in response to a crisis when people realise that the existing format simply doesn't work anymore or it may evolve more organically. Community development helps with these kinds of transitions, beginning with members discussing what's going wrong or what could be done differently.

A familiar situation arises when a community group has achieved or outgrown its original purpose and wishes to take on more ambitious objectives, such as employing staff, taking on a lease or applying for substantial funding. There are a number of options: staying the same with limited aspirations, setting up a new group to pursue the new goals, changing the nature of the group to become more public, possibly linking up with other similar organisations to form some kind of federation or identifying a more established agency – a locally trusted organisation – that can act as the group's accountable body for funding and legal purposes.

Difficulties often occur when members do not recognise the need for change or disagree about the next phase of development. So, for example, a worker might assist a relatively informal group or network to discuss its next steps, to consider alternatives and perhaps agree to become a properly constituted organisation. If the community members decide that they want to set up a formal body, the worker can help them to choose a suitable structure, to establish a clear and common purpose and to decide how any office bearers (chair, secretary, etc.) are going to be democratically elected and held to account. This may involve setting up the organisation as a legal entity in order to safeguard both money and members. Sometimes an organisation needs to grow new structures as the range of its activities expands. For example, a community association might decide to set up a subcommittee to deal with the work it does with young people, or to run an annual event such as a street carnival. As it matures and takes on paid employees, it may find it needs a working group to oversee the recruitment and management of staff.

Providing help, building on resources

Each of these three strands (informal education, collective action and organisation development) involves building the skills, knowledge and confidence of individuals, as well as developing the infrastructure to support community organising and engagement. Community development is sometimes criticised as working from a deficit model: this assumes that communities lack capacity, resources or leadership, and that these need to be either imported from experts or nurtured through 'hand-holding' and training. To a certain extent, this has some resonance with the approach of many professionals, and yet it undervalues the wealth of energy, skills and local knowledge that community members pour into their activities and campaigns. The asset-based model of community development, which is examined later in this chapter, offers a more positive approach (see Kretzmann and McKnight, 1993; Mathie and Cunningham, 2008; Russell, 2015). Nevertheless, there are specific areas of expertise and technical advice that community development workers might provide or refer people to, for example, on charity law, planning regulations or fundraising. In addition, they often have time to do things that community members are too busy to do, or they can offer an external perspective on disputes or difficulties. Encouraging people to reflect on their experiences can be a useful stimulus to further learning and build confidence in new roles. Community workers might make suggestions on group roles and interactions, meetings, the various functions of organisations and the complex dynamics of communities. Their training and accumulated experience can be seen as a resource which is 'on tap' but not 'on top'.

In other words, community workers are there to serve the interests of communities and to help them gain greater influence over decisions that affect their lives. In the early years of community development, there was a vigorous debate over how 'directive' the workers should be, with some arguing that they should be completely neutral, responding entirely to the communities' expressed needs and aspirations, in the ultimate non-directive role (see Batten and Batten, 1967). Some regard this as the highest form of empowerment, leaving communities in control, moving in a direction and at a pace they set themselves. Community development agencies are not always as empowering as they would like to be, and the provision of guidance or advice can be interpreted as overly influential, especially given the relative status and perceived expertise of paid workers. As we will see below and in Chapter Seven, however, there has been acknowledgement that the workers usually do have an agenda, driven to some extent by their employers' policies and priorities, but also by occupational standards and principles (FCDL, 2015). Their work will inevitably be shaped by their own interests, capabilities, preferences and 'theories of change', and it is important that everyone concerned is as honest and 'up-front' about their aims as possible. Transparency and mutual respect should be key values for community development regardless of context or funding arrangements.

Community development's core values

Community development is described as a long-term value-based process. Its overarching purpose is to promote social justice and it is therefore steeped in politics (with a small 'p'). However, social justice is a tricky term to define, tending to mean whatever its proponents want. Within community development, it is usually understood as the development of a fair and inclusive society, with wealth, opportunities and power more equally distributed across the population.

Equality

In practice, this means that community development demonstrates an awareness of the structural inequalities that currently shape society. These are generally associated with class, gender, ethnicity, disability, sexual orientation and age, referring to the most prevalent patterns of discrimination and those covered by the UK's equalities legislation. Equality is a core value for community development, and practitioners are expected to incorporate anti-discriminatory measures into all aspects of their work (Gilchrist, 2007). This means adapting arrangements to take into account the diversity of participants or target communities. Because of its orientation towards social justice, community development is primarily concerned with overcoming and challenging disadvantage. This means that its starting point is supposed problems and deficits, and it is frequently deployed in areas where the whole community is stigmatised and excluded. These might be where there has been social breakdown or long-term failure of the local economy, often in inner cities or peripheral estates, though rural deprivation is also a major issue. Within these populations, there will be further inequalities and tensions caused by different forms of oppression, such as xenophobia or ageism.

Empowerment

Community development places great emphasis on collective leadership, participation and empowerment: community members directly contributing to decision-making about what happens in their areas or spheres of interest. Developing community leadership and people's capacity to influence, and indeed implement, decisions is vital for opening up democratic processes to wider involvement. A recent report from the Commission on Strengthening Local Democracy in Scotland recognises that "building a strong democracy is a journey, and the first step is allowing communities themselves to fully participate in decisions about their own governance" (2014, p 7). It recommends 'significant and systematic re-investment' in community development services to build and redesign local participatory decision making.

Thus community development workers will try to ensure that those who tend to be marginalised in decision making are encouraged to put forward their views and to have these respected. For example, children and young people often find formal meetings alien, so other ways might be found to elicit their ideas and worries, such as using social media platforms, drawing, drama or 'speakeasy' sessions. Levels of empowerment can usefully be envisaged as a ladder or pyramid, with increasing influence for communities depending on the one hand on the actions and attitudes of the 'power holders' and on the other on the confidence, motivation and capacity of the community members involved. As we shall see in Chapter Four, this can range from tokenistic attempts to engage people in 'invited spaces' where the 'rules of the game' and sometimes even the outcomes are already determined, to genuine control of resources and decisions. Community development should aim for communities to be as far towards the 'empowered' or 'in control' end of the spectrum as is feasible in the given circumstances.

Co-operation

As indicated earlier, collective working and co-operation are also key principles of community development, so wherever possible community workers encourage individuals, groups and organisations to work together, informally or through partnership-type arrangements. They may well play a brokering role in making the links between different agencies or parts of the community, identifying potential synergies and mediating latent rivalries or tensions.

Learning together

As a result of community development's commitment to learning and capacity building, it recognises the value of reflection and dialogue. Through informal conversations, workshops and group discussions, community members may develop their ideas of what's happening in their lives or part of the world. Only by understanding how things are now is it possible to change them for the better.

An integrated approach

One model offered for looking at these various principles is to think of community development as way of working *with* communities, which combines six integrated roles (see Table 2.1). In essence, this model is about enhancing the relationship between the people in communities and other partners, including statutory services. It assumes that for communities to gain more influence over decision making and to become more able to design and deliver their own services, they may need external support and advice, as well as securing improvements in how these other agencies are able to listen to and learn from community perspectives.

Related models

The approach described earlier is most commonly practised in the UK, but there are other models that have gained ascendancy and are popular here and in other parts of the world. Several authors have developed useful typologies or frameworks to describe these (Rothman with Tropman, 1970; Smock, 2004; Popple, 2015). Broadly speaking, the categories reflect different analyses of society and different overall goals, with some more radical than others. (See Chapter Four for more detailed explanations of the theory behind these models.) The three approaches described below can be seen as:

(A) fundamentally transforming the way society operates;
(B) rebalancing the system to be fairer and more democratic; and
(C) sharing responsibility for maintaining existing structures and services.

Table 2.1: Six components for community development

Role	Outcome
1. Help people see that they have common concerns about local or other public issues, which they could benefit from addressing together, under their own control	Reduction of isolation and alienation
	Increase in social capital and co-operation
2. Help people to work together on those issues, often by forming or developing an independent community group, supporting them to plan and take actions, and encouraging evaluation and reflection as a way of improving effectiveness	Creation or improvement of bona fide community groups
	Increase in opportunities for activity in the community
	More effective community activity
	Strengthened community sector
	Increase in volunteering
	Mutual aid and autonomous services
3. Support and develop networking between communities and independent groups across the community sector and build links with voluntary sector bodies	Learning between groups
	More effective voice for communities
	Increased 'bridging' social capital and community cohesion
	Improvement in conditions in the locality

Role	Outcome
4. Promote values of equity, inclusiveness, participation and co-operation throughout this work	Increase in: participation social capital collaboration More equal relations and outcomes for disadvantaged communities
5. Empower people and their organisations to influence and transform public policies and services, and other factors affecting the conditions of their lives	Community engagement and influence Improvement in dialogue between communities and authorities Improvement in coherence and effectiveness of public policies
6. Advise and inform public and private authorities on community perspectives and assist them to strengthen communities and work in genuine partnership with them	Increased capacity of agencies, authorities and professions to engage with communities Improvement in delivery of public services Increased resources for the community sector

Adapted from *The Community Development Challenge* report (CLG, 2006, p 17)

(A) Fundamentally transforming the way society operates – radical models

Radical models are concerned with the root causes of injustice and inequality. These approaches are informed by an explanation of power that places it in the hands of elites or those with vested interests, resulting in structural inequalities and systematic discrimination. Perhaps the most well-known is the Alinsky model of community organising, which claims to be broadly oppositional, mobilising communities to confront the 'power holders' in an attempt to negotiate change from a position of collective strength and solidarity (Alinsky, 1972). Alinsky and his disciples operated by building relationships at the grassroots, recruiting and training indigenous leaders to act as organisers, and uniting different parts of communities in alliance around a common cause. For community organisers, the starting point is always the practical concerns and grievances expressed by communities themselves, but the goal may be to redistribute power in favour of disadvantaged people in low income communities, using a pragmatic assessment of ends and means. A frequently adopted tactic is to express mass dissent through protest, often focused on a single person (such as the head of a major polluting industry or a police commissioner), or through imaginative direct actions that expose injustices and demand change. This means engaging with the 'system' from the outside, as well as working within its organisations and structures to challenge how things are done.

> As an organizer I start from where the world is, as it is, not as I would like it to be … It is necessary to begin where the world is if we are going to change it to what we think it should be. (Alinsky, 1972, p xix)

Over recent years, a number of different models of radical community development have evolved in the UK and elsewhere (Beck and Purcell, 2013). Some see these as distinct from traditional community development because they emphasise direct action and informal methods of mobilising. One approach, known as citizen or broad-based organising, draws on Alinsky's model and is used by the Industrial Areas Foundation network in the United States to build alliances of citizens to tackle issues such as low pay or the treatment of asylum seekers. Under the auspices of Citizens UK, it has been highly successful in some of England's bigger cities and runs training for citizens to become community leaders through the Institute for Community Organising.

Another approach to community organising that also emphasises the importance of independent initiatives in civil society was embodied by the government-funded Community Organisers Programme, initially promoted as part of the 'Big Society' agenda. This model, which continues under the Programme's successor body, the Company of Community Organisers (COLtd), underlines the value of listening to residents, building relationships and networks, and mobilising people to take collective action, including community-led events and activities (corganisers.org.uk).

The model of community organising adopted by the government programme was inspired by Freire's writing on popular education (1972). This provides an alternative approach that aims to transform the political basis of society through education and reflective action. Freire's model is based on critical dialogue and has been used to support informal community education among communities that are poor or oppressed. By taking part in facilitated, ongoing conversations, people learn to question what they have been told and become aware of injustices in their lives, as well as possibilities for radical change driven by community action. This process of political awakening has been termed 'conscientisation' and is fundamental to a form of community development that has become known as social pedagogy because it involves shared and experiential learning (Beck and Purcell, 2010). Freirean models are usually associated with a commitment to radical praxis, that is, action based on informed and considered thinking. This approach claims to be transformational in that it aims to create systemic change, challenging prevailing ideologies and leading to an alternative vision for society (Smock, 2004; Ledwith and Springett, 2010; Ledwith, 2015).

(B) Rebalancing the system to be fairer and more democratic – pluralist models

Community development strategies are more often based on liberal pluralist models, which acknowledge that society is made up of an array of interest groups who organise collectively to compete for attention, influence and resources. This approach is concerned with making sure that a full range of experiences and perspectives are taken into consideration when making decisions about how resources are allocated or services designed. It recognises that not all groups have equal access to power and that certain disadvantaged sections of society need additional support and resources in order for their voices and their views to have influence. In this respect, a key role for community development is to address all forms of discrimination and prejudice and attempt to create a more level playing field for members of the community who are oppressed or marginalised. The state is seen as a neutral body, overseeing these negotiations between different interests, with decisions made in accordance with a rational appraisal of the evidence, based on the arguments put forward by diverse stakeholders. The pluralist model of community development aims for reforms that lead to a fairer distribution of power in society generally, as well as at the grassroots.

In some respects, user empowerment falls into this model, whereby service commissioners and providers make available support and mechanisms to enable users to influence delivery and priorities in spending. For example, a social landlord, such as a housing association, might find it expedient to encourage tenants to contribute to decision making about how its properties are managed so that ideas for improvement are captured and there is a greater sense of collective responsibility for the upkeep of the estate, including standards of neighbourly behaviour. There is no question of challenging the ownership and control of the landlord, simply of helping things to run more smoothly in the interests of both parties.

Community engagement represents a parallel model that is open to wider participation and generally not focused on specific services.

It is a stronger version of consultation, by which public authorities seek to involve citizens in planning improvements and addressing longstanding problems. Effective and inclusive engagement practices require changes in the culture and procedures of institutions such as local councils or health authorities to render them more 'community friendly' and accessible. Community engagement strategies *should* result in community and user empowerment, especially if they make use of community development values and expertise.

Both these approaches favour negotiation and compromise rather than conflict. The role of the community development worker, sometimes called participation or engagement officer, is to support community members or service users to develop a collective voice and articulate a persuasive case. To this end, community-led action research can provide evidence to sway the argument. Communities are involved in every aspect of the research process, from deciding the aims, through collecting data, to analysing and presenting the findings. The intention is to demonstrate the impact of particular actions (interventions) and thereby to identify innovative solutions to shared problems. A related approach is known as participatory appraisal. It has been extensively used in the rural areas of countries in the global South (Chambers, 1994) and has been adopted by some organisations in the UK, for example, in the development of village or neighbourhood plans. Essentially, participatory appraisal uses a set of creative, flexible techniques designed to involve as many people as possible in mapping an area's problems, setting priorities and devising solutions. An advantage lies in training community members in these methods so that they can select those most appropriate to the situation and facilitate the process themselves. The role of the agency is to listen, learn and respond to community experiences rather than coming in with preconceived interventions. This allows members of the community to have a greater sense of ownership over proposed strategies, and increases the likelihood that these will work in the particular circumstances and be sustained by the people themselves.

(C) Sharing responsibility to maintain existing structures and services – communitarian models

The third family of community development methods relies on a conservative or functionalist model of society and is more likely to maintain the overall status quo. There is a communitarian emphasis on enabling people to exercise mutual rights and responsibilities without challenging the general order of things. This approach aims to strengthen community spirit and build the capacity of local groups and networks either to contribute independently to civil society or to work in partnership with state or voluntary agencies, perhaps through co-production models. It highlights the positive features of communities rather than their failings, but draws attention to what might happen if communal responsibilities are neglected. Communitarian approaches are designed to mobilise the resources, enthusiasm and efforts of 'ordinary' residents, with one well-known version describing itself as asset-based community development (ABCD) because it focuses on the strengths rather than the weaknesses of communities (Mathie and Cunningham, 2008; Green and Haines, 2015).[1] This comprehensive approach to community building is based on the belief that the role of community development is to assist communities to become self-reliant and cohesive, participating in civil society as a unified body of active citizens. Its foundation is an inventory of individual or household skills, interests and experience to gauge the combined potential capacity of the community, in the belief that:

> Each time a person uses his or her capacity, the community is stronger and the person more powerful. That is why strong communities are basically places where the capacities of local residents are identified, valued and used. Weak communities are places that fail, for whatever reason, to mobilize the skills, capacities and talents of their residents or members. (Kretzmann and McKnight, 2003, p 1)

---

[1]   This model should not be confused with the 'achieving better community development' approach to planning and evaluation, which shares the same acronym (Barr and Hashagen, 2000); see Chapter Seven.

The appreciative enquiry approach offers another set of methods for identifying the positives in community life. It was developed as an alternative to deficit strategies that focus on 'problem solving' and aims to promote creative thinking, whereby people are stimulated to identify all that is good about their communities and encouraged to imagine how things could be 'even better' (Whitney and Trosten-Bloom, 2010).

The ABCD model is interested in assets rather than needs, but, as a consequence, it fails to address the political dimensions that cause needs and problems in the first place. In this it bears a strong resemblance to the civic model proposed by Smock (2004), which she identifies as promoting informal mechanisms for maintaining social order within deprived or diverse neighbourhoods, pre-empting disturbances and attempting to 'bridge' divisions between different sections of the community in the name of stability and consensus. The processes for achieving this could include the establishment of community forums, alongside the development of mediation and conflict resolution skills among key local residents.

Light touch approaches

All of these approaches to working with communities use elements of community development that can be applied with a 'light touch' or within a more general programme of interventions. It is not always necessary to employ a dedicated community development worker for each area to benefit from well-placed advice and encouragement so long as this is available 'on tap' and is responsive to the changing needs of communities themselves (Taylor et al, 2007). On this basis, the Big Local programme in England has adopted a model of 'reps', drawn from a national pool, who provide guidance and support to communities to help them identify local priorities, develop an action plan and form a resident-led strategic partnership.

The skills and strategies used for community development can be applied in various situations and for different purposes. Thus different professional services, such as public health, housing management, youth work, neighbourhood policing, social care, regeneration and so on use community development methods and might be informed to some extent by its values. Chapter Six gives examples of how community development is relevant to a range of policy areas and settings.

Community practice

The term 'community practice' was introduced by Butcher et al (1993). It covers ways of working that recognise that services are delivered most effectively if they are tailored to the conditions and cultures of specific communities. Community practice works at several levels and includes the work of community activists and self-managed groups, as well as paid community workers and other professionals (Banks et al, 2013). It promotes social inclusion and participatory decision making, involving service users, community members, statutory partners and other stakeholders. Community practice is often physically located outside main institutions, for example, in a neighbourhood office or community-owned premises. Thus, it may use a form of outreach or detached service delivery that aims to be more responsive than mainstream services to community needs and preferences. However, most community practitioners have their goals and targets set externally by employers or funders, rather than by the communities themselves. Some critics level the same argument at community development itself, an issue this guide will return to later when we examine challenges around accountability and leadership.

Brief conclusion

Community development is sometimes described as a broad movement for social change. As can be seen from this chapter, in practice it takes many forms and is shaped by different ideologies. What these models have in common is a commitment to working *with* people to remedy situations that are causing injustice, discontent or impoverishment. Despite its rather fuzzy nature as a profession, community development is regularly criticised, rediscovered and adapted by policy makers and governments seeking to achieve long-term improvements in the living conditions of communities that find themselves on the margins of civil society.

Summary

- Community development is about informal learning, collective action and organisational development.
- It is primarily concerned with supporting communities around issues that they identify for themselves but is also used by public, and sometimes private, bodies to improve community engagement.
- Community development aims to increase social justice and works to a number of core values, notably to promote equality, empowerment, co-operation and learning.
- It is useful to consider three different models of community development: radical, pluralist and communitarian.
- As an approach, community development techniques can be adopted by other professions using a light touch to work with communities on their issues and aspirations.

Further reading

There are a number of useful readers on community development, as well as practical guides on working with community groups and on community engagement strategies. The Community Development Foundation produced a range of publications, some of which are now available from the British Library directly as hard copies or to download (via http://socialwelfare.bl.uk/). The national occupational standards for community development work are available from the Federation for Community Development Learning.

Henderson and Vercseg's (2010) exploration of how community development relates to civil society uses interesting examples from the UK and Eastern Europe. Alan Twelvetrees' latest edition of *Community work* (forthcoming) provides a basic text for practitioners. Margaret

Ledwith has authored several thought-provoking books which take a more radical approach, while Akwugo Emejulu (2015) provides a critical comparison of community development in the UK and the US.

Dave Beck and Rod Purcell's (2010) and Carol Packham's (2008) books explore in greater depth the role of the worker in promoting educational aspects of community development, while Beck and Purcell (2013) also offer an overview of models of community organising. More on community organising can be found at www.acorncommunities.org.uk/vtp and www.cocollaborative.org.uk.

For more on asset-based community development, visit www.abcdinstitute.org. Cormac Russell (2015) provides a historical overview while Green and Haines (2015) write about US experiences of this approach.

For an Irish perspective, try Jackson and O'Doherty's (2015) edited collection of case studies and reflections. Jim Ife (2013) with his colleague Tesoriero (2006) brings local and global perspectives to Australian community development practices.

Community Development Alliance Scotland (CDAS) publishes excellent briefings about community development, which can be found at www.communitydevelopmentalliancescotland.org. Community Development Cymru provides the latest information about what's happening in Wales: www.cdcymru.org.

3

the changing policy context

This chapter begins by tracking the way in which community development has evolved over the years and the factors that have shaped this evolution. It then identifies some of the recurrent policy themes that have driven interest in community development and describes the contribution community development can make to these: welfare and service reform, democratic renewal, restoring community, and regenerating places and economies.

How community policies have developed

Origins and early applications

Community development has many foundations in the past. Some lie in communities themselves: the mutual organisations, co-operatives and friendly societies of the eighteenth and nineteenth centuries, for example, where, as industrialisation gained pace, working class people banded together to pool their resources, meet common needs and campaign for improved rights and better conditions. Others can be found in external initiatives, such as the university settlements, mentioned in our introductory chapter. From the 1880s onwards, these brought students into poor urban areas to live and work with local communities. Another is the colonial community development carried out in many countries after World War II to provide a bulwark against communism, to foster economic development in the interests of empire and later deployed to prepare indigenous populations for a peaceful transition to independence. Marj Mayo (1975) traces similar 'colonial' antecedents in the US, where, she argues, self-help projects were supported in order to stave off discontent among black and minority ethnic populations and ensure a skilled and disciplined industrial labour force.

Community development also has roots in the housing and planning fields. The origins of the tenants' movement, for example, lie in campaigns for social housing and rent strikes in the late nineteenth and early twentieth century. They continue with the associations formed by tenants of the new local authority housing estates that were established as the century progressed, which continued to protest against high rents and poor conditions as well as calling for more representation for tenants in housing issues.

The immediate post-war periods saw a wave of housing development, with large-scale slum clearance and reconstruction projects. But the Institute for Community Studies, launched in 1954, compared the soullessness of the post-war new towns and council estates unfavourably with the dense social ties of life in the East London slums from which inhabitants had been moved (Young and Willmott, 1957). Development workers were drafted into these new towns and estates to promote social activities and help build a sense of community (Goetschius, 1969).

At the same time, it was becoming clear that, despite the promise of the post-war welfare state, poverty and disadvantage had not been eliminated. A new wave of dissent was born with the civil rights movement in the US. And towards the end of the 1960s, the flare-up of racial tensions in urban areas triggered government action (Edwards and Batley, 1978). Drawing on the experience of the War on Poverty in the US, the UK government introduced a raft of community initiatives across the country – including the Urban Programme, the National Community Development Project, Education Priority Areas, and the Comprehensive Community Programme.

This policy focus on community was to flounder as the 1970s progressed (although the Urban Programme survived in various guises into the 1990s). In part, and in common with the War on Poverty in the US, this was because of the internal contradictions within the programmes – between the limited aspirations of government and the expectations raised in the populations targeted by these interventions (Marris and Rein, 1967). In part also, it was because these national programmes often encountered resistance from local politicians, while the trenchant critique of capitalism and government policy delivered by the National Community Development Project in the UK undoubtedly sealed its fate (Loney, 1983). Its demise was also hastened by the oil crisis of the early 1970s and the accompanying recession. This signalled the end of the post-war boom, brought rising unemployment and industrial unrest, and prepared the ground for the rise of neoliberalism, with its ideology of shrinking the state in favour of the market. In the UK, community campaigns that had criticised public services now found they had to defend them (Craig et al, 2011). With the election of Ronald Reagan in the US and Margaret Thatcher in the UK, local economic and physical regeneration took centre stage, with the aim of creating jobs and stimulating industrial growth. In some quarters, state support for disadvantaged people was seen as encouraging dependency and the emergence of a 'moral underclass' – a narrative that is only too recognisable in the language of 'strivers and skivers' today.

Although community development was accorded little place in the advance of neoliberalism, it continued to thrive in some areas. In the UK, for example, local authorities opposed to Margaret Thatcher's policies continued to support community development and to address the growing criticism of traditional community development from the women's movement and BME groups. Meanwhile, political emphasis on the consumer role, coupled with the desire to rein in local government, led to a succession of initiatives to engage service users in the design and planning of welfare services. Across the Atlantic, the community development corporations (CDCs) set up in the US in the 1960s grew in number and size. Some US commentators suggest that, as federal funding dried up, CDCs became increasingly entrepreneurial, filling the vacuum left by the withdrawal of the state and departing further and further from their original goals (see, for example, DeFilippis, 2012). By the end of the 1980s, an editorial in the international *Community*

Development Journal was very pessimistic about the prospects for the future (Craig et al, 1990).

The renaissance of community

The 1990s, however, brought the beginnings of a revival. The City Challenge programme in the UK and the Empowerment Zones and Enterprise Communities (EZ/EC) in the US sought to increase economic investment, but also asserted once more the need to involve communities in both the planning and delivery of regeneration programmes. In the UK this was to be the start of a new wave of initiatives that culminated in the National Strategy for Neighbourhood Renewal (NSNR), launched by the New Labour government in 2001. This was a nationwide strategy to tackle social exclusion through investment but also through harnessing mainstream funding for the benefit of the most disadvantaged areas. In England Neighbourhood Renewal Partnerships led by the local authorities serving the most disadvantaged areas brought the public, private and voluntary sectors together to develop and implement strategies that would close the gap between these areas and the rest of the country. Parallel initiatives were established at regional levels and in the devolved administrations of Scotland (Social Inclusion Partnerships) and Wales (Communities First), while in Northern Ireland partnership and community development were integral to the EU PEACE Programme established in response to the Troubles. Community engagement was also a major theme in the European Union's anti-poverty programmes, which were an important source of funding for community development in all four nations, especially in urban and rural areas that had been hard hit by de-industrialisation, such as the loss of mining or manufacturing.

In England the National Strategy's long-term vision of reducing inequalities between the most disadvantaged neighbourhoods and the rest of society was to fade later in the decade. But the commitment to active citizenship and community engagement deepened as part of New Labour's Local Government Modernisation Agenda, with Local Strategic Partnerships – again involving all sectors – replacing Neighbourhood Renewal Partnerships and now covering all areas.

Community engagement was no longer simply 'prescribed for the poor' (Taylor, 2011). It was inherent in the move towards 'localism', a policy theme that, again, was mirrored in the other UK countries. Also common to all four administrations as the 2000s progressed was a growing interest in supporting social enterprise and transferring the management of assets and services to local communities.

Recent developments

These later developments gathered pace with the change of government in the UK from New Labour to a Conservative–Liberal Democrat coalition in 2010 – the first coalition government since World War II. In England the New Labour policy goals of transferring assets to local communities, introducing new community rights, building their capacity to take responsibility for services previously run by the state, and developing the social economy sat well with a neoliberal ideology that was committed to 'rolling back' the state, marketisation and individual and collective self-help. These trends in community policy seemed to be equally prevalent in the other UK countries, despite their different political complexions. Particularly strong has been the intensified search for new ways of funding community-led initiatives that are sustainable and independent of the state. As such, government programmes are no longer the major source of funding for community development that they once were. As state funding has been cut back, the Big Lottery Foundation in particular has become an ever more significant funder across the UK, not only through its open grants programmes but also through programmes like the English and Welsh Big Local and the Northern Ireland Building Change Trust. The latter are delivered through national intermediaries, with timescales of over 10 years and with a strong focus on community control, financial sustainability and long-term transformation.

Another distinct feature post 2010 has been the renewed focus on resident-led approaches. The advent of the Coalition government saw sustained criticism of what was seen as New Labour's 'top-down approach' and its seeming reluctance, despite a rhetoric of localism and empowerment, to devolve power downwards. Community development in particular, was tainted by its perceived co-option into New Labour strategies (Aiken, 2014). Politicians were attracted, on the one hand, by asset-based models – particularly ABCD (see Chapter Two) – and, on the other, by the success of Citizens UK in mobilising large numbers with its radical community organising model (see also Chapter Two). This search for an alternative approach to community development was a feature of the somewhat surprising commitment of the Coalition government – and principally its Conservative partner – to a four-year Community Organisers Programme which would 'train a new generation of community organisers and support the creation of neighbourhood groups across the UK, especially in the most deprived areas' (Cabinet Office, 2010).

For many critics, however, the positive message of what was called 'the Big Society' was more than countered by stringent austerity measures affecting local authorities, voluntary organisations and individuals. Disadvantaged communities faced a perfect storm with harsh cuts in welfare benefits and in public services accompanied by rising levels of unemployment and job insecurity that were to become a feature of the neoliberal economy. Inevitably, this had a knock on effect on the voluntary and community sectors, facing greater demand with less money. Most local government funding now takes the form of contracts for services, subject to the vagaries of competition – a theme we will take up again later.

The community infrastructure in England has suffered particularly badly from cuts at both national and local levels. Government support for the national infrastructure was scaled down in England. As a result, most organisations have been forced to close, although some survive, often through delivering government programmes. In the other UK countries, more has survived and receives some backing from the devolved administrations – in Northern Ireland, for example, a Community Investment Fund continues to support local infrastructure bodies. Meanwhile, the language is very much one of social action and resilience (the latter borrowed from international development), with communities expected to take ever more responsibility for their own survival through self-help, civic engagement, volunteering and corporate match-funding. For many critics, however, current policy is about grooming communities to act as substitutes for the state (NCIA, 2015; Panel on the Independence of the Voluntary Sector, 2015).

International developments

Interest in community development has not, of course, been confined to the US and the UK. We have already noted the emphasis on community engagement in the EU anti-poverty programmes over the years and their importance for many community organisations. Ironically, perhaps, given the criticism that their structural adjustment policies have attracted from some quarters, community participation has also been a feature of the development agendas of the International Monetary Fund and the World Bank. Their programmes often require citizen and community participation, alongside devolution and privatisation, as a condition for financial aid, with community development seen as a tool for democratic restructuring. Many international non-governmental organisations (NGOs) and aid agencies have also supported community development alongside the more immediate demands of disaster response, as a way of creating more sustainable responses to the challenges faced by such communities.

Policy and practice in the global South have increasingly influenced community development thinking in recent decades. There are three reasons for this: the influence of the popular education movement on radical practice, building on the praxis of Paulo Freire (1972; see also Chapter Two, this volume); a response to the democratic innovations that popular movements can bring when they come to power, for example, participatory budgeting in Brazil; and a reflection of the fact that we now live in a globalised world, with significant opportunities for community development to learn across national and regional barriers. We could, of course, argue that globalisation is nothing new. Earlier we referred to the roots of community development in colonialism and its role in supporting imperial economies. But with the hollowing out of the nation state and the revolution in internet-based communication, the implications for community development are now very different.

Information technologies, and specifically social media, have given local communities unprecedented worldwide access to information and contacts, allowing them to network, compare experience and take collective action on a global scale, while new web-based organisations, such as 38 degrees, Avaaz, SumOfUs and GetUp, are seeking ways of combining e-petitions and international campaigns with local action.

Community development policy and practice have also been influenced by another aspect of globalisation, and that is the increasing movement of people across state borders, sometimes willingly but often unwillingly. This affects communities in many different ways. While they may be enriched by the diverse cultures arriving on their doorstep, they may also be prey to inter-ethnic tension and fragmentation, as different ethnic groups seek to preserve their identity. Indeed, over the years racial tensions have been a major trigger for community development initiatives in different parts of the world: community cohesion was a major government priority of the later New Labour years in the UK and policies to combat sectarianism have guided community policy in Northern Ireland and, more recently, Scotland.

Constant themes in community policy

This brief history of the evolution of community development demonstrates the durability of notions of 'community' and community participation, across national boundaries and notwithstanding ideological divisions. So what is the enduring appeal of community over time and to politicians of all persuasions? In the rest of this chapter, we consider four overlapping policy themes from recent years and their implications for community development:

- welfare and public service reform;
- democratic renewal and localism;
- restoring community;
- regenerating local economies.

Welfare and public service reform

Successive governments across the UK have sought to give communities a greater say in the design and delivery of public services, from schools to policing, environmental services and health. Increasingly, however, they look to communities to take over services previously run by the state. Initially, this was most prevalent in the housing field – policies to promote tenant management and control were brought in during the 1990s – but since the beginning of this century, powers have been introduced to allow communities to save local facilities and services threatened with closure and to take over state-run provision, 'where they think they can do so differently and better' (DCLG, 2015, Appendix 3), with various programmes introduced to support them in building the capacity to do so.

Critics claim that these proposals are a mask for the savage cuts in public expenditure that have accompanied austerity, cuts that have hit the poorest communities particularly hard (Beatty and Fothergill, 2013). They argue that opportunities for communities to take over services are more likely to appeal to better off people than residents of low-income neighbourhoods. Given that markets tend to favour scale, it is the larger private companies and the professional voluntary sector (Taylor, 2012) who are most likely to benefit from the opportunity to take over services previously delivered by the state, while procurement practices borrowed from the business world are often ill-suited to the circumstances of small community organisations.

In these circumstances, and despite government's commitment to localism, there is likely in future to be less accountability to, or control by, the users of vital services or the communities in which they are embedded. This has been the case, for example, with the Coalition government's Work Programme, where contracts have been won by large, predominantly private sector partners. In this case, while smaller organisations have been included as potential subcontractors, they find they have either been used as 'bid candy', with little work actually coming through, or they have been subcontracted to work with the most vulnerable clients at unsustainable rates, bearing the associated costs and risks without adequate return.

It would, however, be a mistake to see a move to community-run services solely as an external imposition. Many people in the most disadvantaged communities have suffered over the years from poor facilities and inadequate, stigmatising services with high staff turnover. There are a growing number of examples where residents have successfully run their own services and facilities (Wind-Cowie, 2010; Aiken et al., 2011). And there is interest from government and communities in forms of co-production, whereby the resources and knowledge of different sectors and players can be pooled (Pestoff and Brandsen, 2008; Durose and Richardson, 2015). In addition, people in communities have often provided informal support and neighbourly help to each other. With rising levels of need, this will become ever more necessary. The danger is, however, that volunteering ceases to become a choice and becomes a necessity – indeed, for those in or seeking work, it may become a requirement for continuing to receive certain benefits, a form of US-style workfare.

So what are the implications of these trends for community development? It clearly has a vital contribution to make in supporting those who do want to take advantage of the new opportunities to run services, manage assets or promote volunteering, and to ensure that they are adequately resourced to do so. However, there are many who simply want 'decent' and responsive services without having to run them themselves. And there are others who do not have the resources or confidence to do so – some communities and population groups have many more assets than others. In this context, community development has a particular role to play in helping residents to defend the services that they need and to hold providers to account, ensuring that services and facilities, whoever runs them, are accessible, equitable and accountable.

Democratic renewal and localism

As world institutions seek to extend democracy across the world, voting figures in the more established democracies have been falling for decades in national and local elections. Active membership of the main UK political parties has declined markedly. Generally speaking, here and elsewhere, the public appears to have become increasingly disillusioned with the way formal politics is carried out.

In our first edition, published in 2011, we suggested that there were a variety of reasons for this, from small- and large-scale political corruption to the changing circumstances of contemporary life. Mass institutions no longer have the appeal they once did and governing elites seem more and more distant from the man or woman on the street. In the UK, for example, the national politician who has made his or her way up through local government or even a 'real job' seems an increasing rarity. Social media platforms are changing the nature of politics too, spreading opinion and information and opening up debate. All these factors appear to have created a crisis of legitimacy for representative democracy.

Since our first edition, however, the picture has changed. The Scottish referendum achieved a turnout of 84.5%, higher than any general election in the UK since 1918. And, while membership of the UK main political parties was at an historic low prior to the 2015 general election (Keen, 2015), numbers belonging to, and voting for, the smaller parties had risen markedly. But, after the election – which returned a Conservative government to sole power – both the main opposition parties experienced a surge in membership, with Labour membership the highest since 1997. Most tellingly, the search for new leader of the Labour Party in England after its defeat was galvanised by the entry – and subsequent election of – a candidate from the Left who was seen as radically different from the political elite. His rallies and social media presence attracted a considerable following, particularly among young people, and it is becoming clear that there is indeed a well of interest to be tapped – though perhaps not in conventional ways.

From the 1990s onwards, the response of governments across the world to the need for democratic reform has been a well-documented move from 'government' to more participative forms of 'governance', with the growth of partnership working (see Chapter Four). The language of citizen participation has been everywhere, promoted by supranational institutions like the World Bank and the European Union (EU), as well as national governments around the world. The EU, for example, made the promotion of participatory democracy a key objective and introduced a Citizens' Initiative that allows one million citizens from a number of member states to call on the Commission to bring forward new policy proposals. It also set up a Citizens' Agora, which brings citizens, civil society organisations and elected politicians together to debate key challenges for the EU.

As part of this move, national and local governments have introduced new partnership and participatory mechanisms and there is a thirst for innovatory methods of deliberative democracy. In England the New Labour government included empowerment in the set of national indicators it introduced as part of the settlement between central and local government in the early 2000s, with a measure of the 'percentage of people who feel they can influence decisions in their locality'. Programmes were introduced here and in other parts of the UK to support community involvement in the strategic partnerships that were set up at local authority level. In more recent years, the emphasis has changed to co-production and community ownership – as the previous section indicated – while in the voluntary sector more widely, contractual relationships with the state appear to be taking over from partnership working. But in some fields (notably health, see Chapter Six) and in some localities interest in partnership and participation remains. In Scotland, for example, the Community Empowerment Act 2015 puts Community Planning Partnerships on a statutory footing and includes powers that require Scottish public authorities to promote the participation of the public in the decisions and activities of the authority, including in the allocation of its resources. The Scottish government has also taken a strong interest in participatory budgeting, with training offered to all public authorities in Scotland.

Partnership working has proved something of a mixed blessing. The 'invited spaces' (Cornwall, 2004) in which communities and citizens have been encouraged to participate have often been shaped and controlled by the power holders rather than communities themselves and, as we have seen, partnership policies have been criticised for co-opting those who participate in them, diverting communities from identifying and pursuing their own priorities. For critics, therefore, the recent move in England away from partnership working provides an opportunity for community action to rediscover its soul (Taylor, 2012). After all, independent community action has a long tradition, with communities running their own campaigns and claiming their own 'popular spaces' for change.

However, many of the more traditional working class organisations, where citizens found a common voice, gained a political education and established their collective strength, have disappeared. Political parties, trade unions, adult education institutes and social clubs, for example, no longer have a presence in many local neighbourhoods, nor are they able to inspire solidarity very far beyond their membership. Against this, there are new forms of collective action and politics – particularly through the internet and social media – for community development to engage with.

What are the implications for community development? This is an approach that has long supported those who want, or need, to take collective action around a shared issue. That support will continue to be necessary wherever people wish to tackle local issues, get organised and gain influence. Community development has a significant role to play, too, in cultivating new 'popular spaces' to replace – or revive – those that have gone, creating opportunities for dialogue and debate which can encourage political awareness and confidence among the most disadvantaged citizens. Meanwhile, more radical approaches can bring communities together, in and across localities and regions, to challenge current trends and policy developments and create the momentum for change, as organisations like Citizens UK have shown. At the same time, working from inside the system, community development needs to work with external actors – public and private –

to raise their awareness and capacity to engage meaningfully with communities.

Restoring community

'Community lost' has been a strong theme of social commentary since the industrial revolution, and this concern has been reflected in policy debates. In the 1990s a strong communitarian lobby emerged based in part on a perceived breakdown in moral consensus, social cohesion and civic responsibility. This was attributed to a loss of 'social capital', a concept popularised by Robert Putnam (1993) to describe the networks, norms and trust associated with well-functioning communities and civil society (for further discussion, see Chapter Four). Some blamed this breakdown on the dependency created by state welfare; others saw the individualism of the market as the villain of the piece, giving rise to increasing fragmentation and eroding the public sphere. The theme of a 'broken society' has been a favourite of politicians over the centuries and persists to the present day, regardless of the evidence.

Other factors pose a challenge to traditional notions of community. As we shall explore further in Chapter Eight, communities are increasingly made up of people with multiple allegiances and divergent cultures. At the same time, the ageing of the population can result in intergenerational tensions, while changing patterns of tenure can lead to social fragmentation as people move more often and are able to devote less time to putting down local roots.

The recent recession and the austerity policies that have followed it have had a devastating effect on areas that have already lost the industries that shaped them and are now, as we have seen, the hardest hit by the impact of public spending cuts on jobs and services (Beatty and Fothergill, 2013). Housing benefit cuts mean that families are being displaced from more affluent areas and rehoused often miles away with the inevitable disruption of communities and relationships. The rise of private renting, with inadequate regulation, also contributes to instability, with families, and especially young people, in expensive and insecure tenancies.

It is also the most disadvantaged areas that are most likely to be expected to absorb new populations – where asylum seekers, or those families who are displaced from more affluent areas, are housed. And yet there is often little support for the communities most affected by population change. There is concern, too, that inter-ethnic hostility is often fanned by the feeling in host communities that they have been abandoned (Beider, 2011). Newcomers are often blamed for circumstances beyond their control (Taylor and Wilson, 2015). As a result, more attention and effort is needed to increase mutual understanding among diverse residents who do find themselves sharing the same neighbourhood, even if this is temporarily or reluctantly,

Robert Putnam's argument about social capital, which resonated strongly with policy makers throughout the world, was that it underpinned democracy and boosted economic development. It has since been linked with a range of other positive outcomes (Halpern, 2005; see also Chapter Four, this volume). 'Restoring community' can thus be seen as the foundation stone to the other policy themes discussed here. Without basic community development at local level, other interventions are unlikely to be adequately rooted. On the other hand, this should not obscure the need for policies to address the structural and economic factors that marginalise significant sections of the population.

Over the years there have been numerous programmes designed to 'restore community'. Civil renewal and 'active citizenship' initiatives seek to support volunteering, civic engagement, self-help and neighbourliness, encouraging people to look out for one other, promoting resilience and 'bonding' social capital. These tend to be a constant whatever the ideological persuasion of government, although there is less evidence for their effectiveness (Ishkanian and Szreter, 2012). Meanwhile, 'community cohesion' and similar policies seek to connect communities and build bridging social capital across races, faiths, generations and other potential fault lines. Concern with the rise of the far Right in Europe and the effects of violent extremism has also led to debate about the alienation of the white working class and to the introduction of programmes to tackle this. However, anti-extremism policies can also have the effect of diminishing trust.

Again, it is important to recognise that communities do not wait for external initiatives to bring them together formally. This is the stuff of everyday, often informal, community action (Richardson, 2008). But in fractured and neglected neighbourhoods, where social bonds have been eroded by factors far outside the residents' control, or in neighbourhoods where individual and family survival takes up enormous amounts of energy, community development has an important role in supporting this basic activity and reducing isolation and suspicion.

Regenerating places and economies

Poverty is not confined to specific localities. However, it is concentrated in particular neighbourhoods – often in areas of social housing. These neighbourhoods – the ones that economic changes have left behind – have been the focus of many area-based initiatives over the past 50 years or so.

Community development has had a close relationship with planning and housing policy – both in disadvantaged areas and more generally. The Coalition government post 2010 took action to reform the planning system in England to give local people more opportunities to shape the places in which they live, while neighbourhood and community planning continue to attract government support elsewhere in the UK. Community development has also had a role to play to support communities in opposing plans that have gone against the wishes of the community. Recent examples include proposals to demolish existing communities in order to build upmarket housing for investment, or to resist the take-over of local high streets by supermarkets. Similar campaigns were common in the 1970s, too, as residents fought against schemes to demolish their homes to make way for redevelopment.

A feature of early initiatives such as the US War on Poverty and the UK Community Development Projects was their holistic approach, and this was also the case with the various neighbourhood renewal/ social inclusion and peace initiatives in the different UK countries in the early 2000s, as well as several EU-funded programmes. But in between times the focus turned to physical regeneration and to reviving local economies so that they would become 'working neighbourhoods', with an emphasis on job creation and community economic development. This economic emphasis has now returned – at least in England and Wales.

Current policy promotes the transfer of assets – buildings, public spaces and so on – to communities, alongside the development of local social enterprises. Both strategies help people to gain a sense of place, as well as helping to preserve local heritage and regenerate local economies. We referred earlier to the highly successful community development corporation movement in the US. While slower to take off in England, this transfer of assets has grown appreciably over the past 10 years or so, partly as the result of 'endowments' from major regeneration initiatives that transfer the ownership of social housing to tenant management organisations, partly through the enterprise of residents themselves, and partly through community economic development initiatives. Governments the world over are also promoting forms of 'social innovation' that combine social with commercial goals to contribute to a 'double' or even 'triple' bottom line (economic, social and environmental). The current interest in social investment and enterprise can draw on a strong and innovative body of experience in community economic development in the global South, as well as the social economy tradition in Europe. We will return to this and its implications for community development in Chapter Six.

Brief conclusion

Community development has a long history in public policy and practice as part of the wider and longstanding interest in the idea of 'community'. Successive governments across the world have sought to strengthen community ties, build community capacity and resilience, and 'restore community'. Communities have been seen as a crucial resource in policies to reform services, to revitalise democracy and to regenerate local environments and economies. But critics argue that communities are being used to further a neoliberal agenda, which undermines the public sphere. Community development can support communities to make full use of new opportunities, while ensuring that they meet real community needs, are available to all communities and are not open to exploitation. It also has an important role to play in building links with policy makers and other external actors to ensure that opportunities are developed in dialogue with communities and supported by policies that address the wider causes of exclusion and inequality.

Summary

- Community development has come in and out of fashion as policies change, but since the beginning of the 1990s, 'community' and community participation have been promoted by international institutions as well as national governments of varying political and ideological persuasions.
- Community development has been influenced by popular movements, from the civil rights movement of the 1960s to global campaigns in the twenty-first century.
- Policy interest in community development has been driven by the desire to reduce the role of the state and to give service users a greater say in welfare provision and local planning.
- Community development has also been promoted as a means of addressing the democratic deficit, through increased citizen participation and community engagement and through devolving powers from central government.
- A third factor has been concern over the fragmentation of community life and a perceived loss of 'social capital'.
- Community development has a central role to play in the regeneration of neighbourhoods that have suffered from the collapse of traditional industry and the ever-present spatial concentration of poverty.

Further reading

Several books on community development provide a historical account. Students will find the community development readers mentioned in the previous chapter particularly useful in this respect (see also Taylor, 2011; Popple, 2015). Those who are interested in learning from history (rather than repeating it) will find much of interest in the classic texts by Peter Marris and Martin Rein (1967) on the US War on Poverty, and Martin Loney (1983) on the National Community Development Project, as well as the work now being carried out to study the legacy of the CDPs through the Imagine research project: (www.imaginecommunity.org.uk/projects/the-historical-context). Readers may also be interested in a new series from Policy Press – Rethinking Community Development – which looks at the challenges facing community development today.

4

theoretical concepts

This chapter examines some of the theoretical perspectives and concepts that inform community development, its understanding of the context within which it works and the potential for social change. These include theories of community, social capital and collective efficacy; the state, democracy and power; institutional and complexity theory; and social movement theory.

What theory offers

Community development has values – primarily of social justice and democracy, for example – but these tell us what it is trying to achieve, not how it might do so. Theories help us to understand why and how facts and events come to be as they are, and provide an analytical framework to guide our judgements and actions.

Theories from a variety of different disciplines can help community development to understand the world in which it intervenes and community workers may use different theories of change to decide which strategies to pursue. There are theories that help to explain how communities work (or not), how power works, how policies are made, how people can be mobilised and what motivates them, how collective action can be organised, and how systems operate and adjust to change. There are theories of 'social change', of democracy, of the state. There are also theories of civil society, associations, relationships and networks. Economics, sociology, human geography, and psychology and management theories all have something to offer to our understanding of community and community development.

Finding a way through this wide array of theoretical approaches is a lifetime's work. Certainly, in a book of this size, it is impossible to do justice to the theories that might prove useful to the student or practitioner of community development. In this chapter we set out some of the key ideas that we have found most helpful, offering a brief guide, but we recommend that readers follow our signposts to further reading. In other chapters we have developed theory about practice itself, generally referred to as praxis.

We start by exploring the concept of community and associated theories of social capital. We then discuss some psychological concepts that can offer an understanding of the processes involved in community development as well as ideas about individual motivation and collective efficacy. We move on to theories of the state and of democracy, since these are the context within which community development operates. The next section broadens the discussion out to consider theories of power and what they can tell us about the relationship between 'structure' and 'agency', that is, how much of what communities do and experience is determined for them and how much they can determine for themselves. We then briefly consider how a fourth family of theories – about systems and institutions – help us to understand more about the structures that promote or prevent change. In our final section we visit some aspects of social movement theory, to learn about opportunities for change and how to mobilise people for collective action. In each section, we highlight the implications for community development.

Theories of community

'Community' can mean many different things. One study in the mid-twentieth century (Hillery, 1955) found 94 definitions of community, and the most that could be agreed on was that community involves social interaction and some common ties or bonds. Community can simply be a description of a set of people who share some characteristics. Or it can be used normatively to suggest how communities *should* operate, for example, with community as a site of moral cohesion, where people trust each other and are prepared to help each other out. It can also be used instrumentally to suggest agency, implying that communities can act together to achieve common ends or implement government policies (Butcher et al, 1993; Day, 2006; Taylor, 2011). Often the three uses are confused, leading commentators to deplore the use of community as an 'empty signifier' – a word without meaning in the real world (Somerville, 2011).

While the discussion so far might lead us to search for a definition of community that is free from normative and instrumental connotations, Raymond Plant suggests that this is unlikely to be achieved, arguing that '[c]ommunity is so much part of the stock in trade of social and political argument that it is unlikely that some non-ambiguous and non-contested definition of the notion can be given' (1974, p 12).

Plant tracks interest in community back to German sociological thought in the late eighteenth and early nineteenth centuries – a time of growing concern about rapid industrialisation and its impact on society. This concern was captured in the distinction that Ferdinand Tönnies made later in the nineteenth century between *Gemeinschaft* and *Gesellschaft*, or Durkheim's definitions of organic and mechanical solidarity, both of which contrasted the traditional territorial communities often associated with rural life with the newer fragmented, contractual relationships that characterised industrialised urban society.

The ties of community were also contrasted with the impersonality of the state. Robert Nisbet (1953), for example, drew on nineteenth century German traditions to argue for the importance of community as a critical mediating institution between state and citizen. Others have seen 'community' as an alternative to the state, a view promoted in the 1990s by the communitarian movement, referred to in previous chapters. Spearheaded by Amitai Etzioni, communitarianism became influential in many policy circles at that time. Strongly normative, it emphasises respect for others as well as self-respect, responsibilities as well as rights, self-government and service to others, with the family first and then the community as the sites in which moral norms and obligations are developed (Etzioni, 1998). As we saw earlier, the communitarian influence remains evident in current policies that support communities in taking collective action and running services for themselves. However, as Thornham and Parry point out (2015), this is potentially undermined by a parallel emphasis in neoliberal ideology on individual responsibility and entrepreneurialism.

The early 1990s also saw the introduction of another highly influential concept into the community portfolio. 'Social capital' can trace its roots back to the early twentieth century, but was introduced into popular debate in the 1990s through the work of Robert Putnam. He defined it as 'features of social life – network, norms and trust – that enable participants to act together more effectively to pursue shared objectives' (Putnam, 1993, pp 664–5) and lamented its decline in the US, arguing that relationships of trust were crucial to making local economies and democracy work. The World Bank reflected this view, referring in 1999 to social capital as the 'glue' that holds society together (see: http://go.worldbank.org/K4LUMW43B0). High levels of social capital have been linked with greater productivity, effective democracy, better health, safer communities, higher educational achievement and a host of other positive effects (see, for example, Halpern, 2005).

Like 'community', social capital is a contested term, capable of many interpretations. Some theorists, including Putnam and James Coleman (1990), regard social capital as a collective resource on which individuals can draw. Others see it as an individual resource (Portes, 1995) and, as such, Bourdieu (1986) argued that the access to the resources it provided was as inequitably distributed as any other form of capital, thus reinforcing existing divisions and privileges in society. Later commentators have criticised the tendency of social capital's champions to confuse the concept of social capital with the positive outcomes it is supposed to deliver and overlook its so-called 'dark side'. Networks can be exclusive, secretive and unaccountable. Social norms can be oppressive for some, and trust is a hugely complicated idea, dependent on individual connections and social contexts.

Close ties can foster discrimination and conservatism, causing social stagnation and resistance to change (Portes, 1995; Burns and Taylor, 1998; Sampson, 2004).

Some of these concerns have been addressed by Michael Woolcock (1998) and others, in their distinction between different forms of social capital: bonding, bridging and linking:

- Bonding social capital describes enduring strong relations between people in similar situations, such as close friends and family.
- Bridging social capital describes weaker relationships between people who are different in their social identity or location, such as connections that span the boundaries between different ethnic groups or communities of interest.
- Linking social capital describes connections between people that cut across status and link people with differing levels of power: service users and service providers, for example, or community members and government officials.

While bonding social capital is good for 'getting by', bridging and linking social capital are needed for 'getting on' or 'getting ahead'. This distinction between bonding and bridging builds on work by Mark Granovetter (1973), who argued that, when it came to seeking employment, strong ties were less useful than a large and more diverse network of weaker ties. Similarly, Wellman (1979) has argued that weaker ties may provide indirect access to a greater variety of resources than stronger, more socially homogeneous ties. However, Somerville (2011, p 60) argues that each form of social capital can be associated with social divisions and inequalities, while the development of formal bridging (and indeed linking) social capital may loosen the more informal strong ties of bonding.

So what does this mean for community development? Distinguishing between different forms of social capital is particularly important in this field because social change cannot be achieved simply by working at community level on small-scale projects or local campaigns. Bridging and linking social capital are needed to harness resources and influence beyond the community, to connect with allies and broader social movements (Ledwith and Springett, 2010). And while many disadvantaged communities are characterised by strong ties (they can 'get by'), they are often poorly connected with those outside their boundaries, whether other communities or power holders, whose resources and opportunities may help them to 'get ahead' (McCabe et al, 2013).

But what will translate these ties into effective collective action? To answer this question, we need to take a brief step sideways into questions of group behaviour, experiential learning, individual motivation and collective efficacy.

Psychological concepts and theories

Group dynamics, experiential learning and motivation

Since community development is primarily concerned with enabling people to work together for social change, it is crucial to understand what prompts individuals to become involved and how they relate to others. Psychology, the study of mind and behaviour, provides some useful insights and theories about human development, decision making, learning and emotions. It can also help us to understand how relationships develop through increasing disclosure, growing trust and changing interpersonal perceptions (Duck, 2007). Exploration of group dynamics reveals the range of roles that different people choose, depending on personality traits, preferred emotional styles or skills sets (see, for example, Belbin, 2009). This can affect how leadership evolves and also how conflicts are dealt with (or not). Tuckman's (1965) model of group development suggests that all groups go through at least four stages, labelled 'forming, storming, norming and performing', and this can be useful in recognising that tensions and disagreements are to be expected during the early phases of getting going, rather than being a major crisis. Since Tuckman's model was first published, other stages have been added, including 'adjourning' and 'mourning', which helpfully reflect the endgames that some groups inevitably reach and which must be carefully handled.

As indicated in Chapter Two, community development is concerned with informal learning that builds on experience and existing knowledge, leading to new capabilities and different ways of seeing the world. Kolb's (1984) theories of experiential learning propose that learning from experience involves a continuous cycle of action, learning and reflection, during which people interact with their environment, and receive input from other people. He shows how different learning styles can help to shape the way in which community members share knowledge, question received opinion and develop their own ideas and confidence. This dynamic 'sense-making' process is related to Freire's model of social pedagogy and can also be applied to team situations to optimise how people work together to solve problems and achieve shared goals.

Obviously, learning is not always linear or straightforward – it may involve sudden insights and shifts in awareness, especially when different people with very different views are involved. Changes in attitude often involve a period of 'cognitive dissonance', whereby a person's views are at odds with their behaviour. This can be the case for example, where prejudices and assumptions are being challenged, when strong emotions can obscure evidence and logical thinking. So acknowledging how emotions influence perceptions and decision making is also important (Hoggett et al, 2009). Community development needs to work with the grain of feelings and expectations – harnessing hopes, compassion and loyalties to craft common purpose, while simultaneously handling their more negative counterparts, for instance, anger, fear and envy.

There are a number of theories about decision making: how people weigh up options and are influenced by external factors, such as other people's opinions or resource limitations. Some people are more inclined to take risks, while others prefer to play it safe, keeping within known certainties. Nudge theory (Thaler and Sunstein, 2008) takes forward Kahneman's and Tversky's thinking on behavioural economics (Kahneman and Tversky, 2000) and is used to explain how the choices people make can be influenced, for example, around registering to become organ donors or paying taxes. In a nutshell, it aims to redesign the 'choice architecture' facing people so that their own choices are aligned with those that are considered to be in their best interests. In the UK the government has been influenced by this approach and currently applies 'nudge theory' to influence behaviour of citizens in a variety of ways (Halpern, 2015). This can be seen as manipulation and there is a fine line to be drawn, but since community development work usually involves working with people who are volunteering their time and energy, nudge theory might help community development workers to think about how to encourage participation and collective action in the context of local customs and circumstances.

This brief account offers a partial introduction to psychological aspects of community development. The interested reader might want to explore other relevant concepts relating to communication, individual differences, life stages, attribution theory, social identity and collective efficacy.

Understanding motivation and efficacy

Some models of motivation argue that people's behaviour can be explained as a rational strategy to maximise personal benefits and minimise costs in response to patterns of probable rewards and incentives. However, this is widely criticised as too simplistic and ignores the complexity of factors that motivate people. One theory with which most community development workers will be familiar is that of Abraham Maslow (1943). Maslow argues that there is a hierarchy of needs that starts with basic physiological requirements, and then moves through security and safety, belongingness, self-esteem and recognition, to self-actualisation. Self-actualisation, he argues, is only attainable if the layers of need below it have been satisfied. However, this has been criticised as being culturally biased towards Western, individualistic societies (Hofstede, 2001).

Albert Bandura's theory of self-efficacy explores further the factors that determine how people behave in specific situations. He defines self-efficacy as people's beliefs about their capabilities to behave in such a way that will 'exercise influence over events that affect their lives' (Bandura, 1994, p 1). He argues that these beliefs are the result of social processes and have four main sources:

- experience (success increases self-efficacy; failure lowers it);
- social modelling (if s/he can do it, so can I);
- social persuasion (encouragement not only in terms of positive appraisals but also in structuring situations so that people are likely to succeed);
- physical and emotional factors and how they are perceived.

It is easy to see from this list how circumstances and experiences might undermine people's self-efficacy. Individuals will be less likely to engage in any kind of collective action if their life experience does not instil confidence in their ability to succeed, if they have few models of success around them, or if engaging in any kind of public action makes them feel anxious, angry or insecure (Taylor, 2011). Nor will they feel confident enough to take part if they are rarely encouraged or put in a situation where they can succeed.

The concept of collective efficacy, as developed by Robert Sampson and others (Sampson, 2004), is rooted in self-efficacy. But Sampson is critical of policies that focus on the individual. In this he is in agreement with social capital theory, stressing the importance of personal ties, co-operation and social interaction. His study of crime prevention in Chicago (Sampson et al, 2002) observed that the neighbourhoods which seemed to have low rates of vandalism and less serious crime were those where residents appeared to have strong social networks and believed that by working together they could make things happen. The study found more social interaction on the streets in these areas and evidence of community-level organisations working to tackle local issues.

Networks are only part of the explanation for collective efficacy, however. Sampson's research focuses on the conditions that link interpersonal ties and trust with shared expectations for action. He argues that networks have to be activated to be meaningful and that 'dense tight-knit networks may actually impede social organisation, if they are isolated or weakly linked to collective expectations for action' (2007, p 168). He also underlines the importance of 'a strong institutional infrastructure', where the legitimacy of social order comes in part from mutual engagement and negotiation among residents, local institutions and agencies of law enforcement (p 113), thus emphasising what social capital theorists would call linking as well as bonding and bridging ties. As part of this infrastructure, his research stresses not only the importance of participation in grassroots community organisations but also the presence of neighbourhood services. Sampson is critical of policies that undermine trust, including zero tolerance and mass imprisonment. He also highlights the negative impact of structural inequalities on collective efficacy. 'Inequality in resources', he argues, 'matters greatly for explaining the production of collective efficacy' (2004, p 108).

The relevance of community development in promoting self- and collective efficacy seems clear. Community workers can help to create Bandura's conditions for self-efficacy by giving people the opportunity for positive experiences that will build their confidence: helping them identify the factors that led to success or failure, putting them in touch with groups which have been successful, offering encouragement, and giving them opportunities to discuss how they feel about experiences of success or failure. They can also build the links between communities and external organisations that Sampson identifies as essential to social stability and local control (Sampson, 2007, p 169). But efficacy does not just depend on the conditions people create for themselves. To understand more about the relationship between disadvantaged communities and external players, we need now to consider theories of the state.

Theories of the state and the process of government

Much community development in the immediate post-war era in the UK operated on the basis of encouraging people in disadvantaged neighbourhoods to build 'community' and to organise to help themselves. It also worked with local service providers to make them more responsive to need. But this approach was rejected in the 1970s by workers in the UK Community Development Projects (CDPs), who described it as 'gilding the ghetto'. Adopting a class analysis, they placed the responsibility for the plight of disadvantaged communities not with their residents but with the state as the instrument of capitalism, highlighting the disappearance of financial investment, jobs and manufacturing from these areas and describing how government subsidies (for example, in housing policy) favoured the middle classes – a critique paralleled in the US (O'Connor, 2012).

Marxist theories

The CDP critique was derived mainly from Marxist theory, which argues that the political and cultural arrangements in any given society are determined by the relations, means and forces of production. Because the economic cycles of capitalism inevitably generate conflict between the classes, Marx argued that capitalism contained inherent contradictions and thus, he argued, the 'seeds of its own destruction'. Change would come when the oppressed class rose up against the bourgeoisie and placed the means of production under collective ownership, allowing the state to wither away.

Some would argue that history has proved this prediction wrong but others still find Marxist economic analysis helpful in understanding today's versions of capitalism (Chang, 2010; Piketty, 2013). Some of the most influential theory for community development over the years was to come instead from other thinkers in the Marxist stable, notably Antonio Gramsci and Paulo Freire. Gramsci, for example, was critical of Marxist economic determinism and focused instead on the ideological apparatus of the capitalist state. He introduced the idea of 'hegemony' to explain how dominant ideologies pervade society and become accepted as common sense:

> Whereas coercion is exercised overtly through the armed forces, the police, the courts and the prisons, consent is subtly woven in through the institutions of civil society – the family, schools, the media, political parties, religious organisations, cultural, charitable and community groups – in a way that permeates our social being and asserts hegemonic control by influencing our ideas. (Ledwith, 1997, pp 122–3)

Marxism is one of a set of theories that argues that power is held by certain groups or forces in society. In particular, it characterises society as based on class conflict, with different sections inextricably caught up in opposition due to their competing interests. Other 'conflict' models include theories of elite domination, patriarchy and structural racism. A further group of theories, while less antagonistic, has explored the way in which actors within the state maximise their own interests – these range from public choice theory to theories of bureaucracy and policy networks.

Community groups on their own are unlikely to have the resources or institutional capacity to counter these dominant forces. As indicated in Chapter Two, radical models of community development have promoted strategic alliances between disadvantaged communities and the labour movement. Community development has also turned to the discourse and critical dialogue models of Gramsci and Freire as a means of raising the consciousness of the powerless in order to challenge existing hegemonies and forms of systemic power. Instead of Marxist revolution, Gramsci saw change as coming through education, cultural shifts and the formation of social movements. He argued that radical consciousness is developed through informed debate, ideas that were to be developed by Paulo Freire in Latin America through an approach termed 'critical pedagogy' (see Chapter Two). Gramsci highlighted the importance of outside 'political educators' as catalysts for change, but he also championed the role of 'organic intellectuals', who remain culturally rooted in communities, combining knowledge and ideas with direct experience of class oppression (Ledwith, 2011).

Pluralist theories

Pluralist theories of the state challenge the deterministic view adopted by conflict models. They understand power as something that is dispersed throughout society, with democratic decision-making based on advocacy and negotiation between different interests. A pluralist analysis sees the state as playing a mediating role: setting standards and upholding rights that protect the freedom of groups to further their political interests, while preventing any one group from doing harm or undermining the liberty of others. In this view, the role of community development is to support disadvantaged communities in making their voices heard and in becoming politically active, so as to increase their bargaining power.

Traditional pluralism has been criticised for its failure to acknowledge the imbalance of power between different interests in society or indeed to recognise tendencies towards oligarchy, whereby decision making remains with the few. Pluralist theory also fails to acknowledge the way that dominant hegemonies structure the operation of power. Jürgen Habermas, for example, is critical of the dominance of 'instrumental rationality' in society (Habermas, 1984). He argues for new forms of 'communicative action', which can confront the distortion of reality by the powerful and transform power relationships.

There are a number of implications for community development here. It can work with communities to develop their confidence and voice, so that they can organise effectively, create their own narratives, assert their interests and challenge prevailing hegemonies. It can work with power holders to build their capacity to engage in more equal dialogue with communities. It can also help to create opportunities for communities to express and negotiate disagreements. However, reviewing critiques of pluralism, Popple (2015) reminds us that the local and empiricist approaches that are derived from a pluralist analysis can be placatory and are unlikely to lead to significant change.

Governance theories

Governance and regime theorists also adopt a pluralist, multi-agency approach. They argue that in today's complex and fragmented society it is not possible for the state to govern on its own. Instead regimes are formed which bring new resources and knowledge into decision-making circles. While regimes can still be relatively closed, the governance discourse highlights the potential for government to 'steer' and to open up its decision making to greater participation and more widespread deliberation. In this way, Gerry Stoker has argued, governance networks do not just influence policy, they take over the business of government (Stoker, 1998, p 23). However, critics argue that the networks of governance, like many other networks, tend to be biased, opaque and unaccountable. The structure of society still privileges certain actors over others.

The literature on policy networks, however, suggests that there are different kinds of networks in the governance process, not all of which are closed. Sabatier (1988), for example, argues that the policy subsystem is composed of a number of 'advocacy coalitions' that compete for influence and for the attention of 'policy brokers'. While these coalitions are unlikely to influence the core beliefs of governing regimes, they can influence the way in which problems are framed and the detail of plans to achieve common goals. Thus the interest shown by successive governments in community engagement could be seen to give more disadvantaged groups an entrée into policy making circles, bringing knowledge, legitimacy and access to groups whose voices are seldom heard.

This strand of theory suggests that there are opportunities for communities and those who work with them to influence policy to their advantage and to have 'agency'. If these opportunities are to be grasped, however, community development workers need to understand the dynamics of policy making, help groups to gain access to policy makers, and find allies within and outside the system. Increasingly, in today's society, this will mean identifying those other interests beyond the state that influence policy and resource distribution in a globalised capitalist system. It also requires an understanding of how power might work.

Theories of power: structure or agency?

Community development is concerned with promoting social justice, equality and inclusion. An understanding of power is therefore critical to effective practice, recognising the different ways in which power is denied to communities, but also the potential for communities to generate their own forms of power and shape the way power operates.

How power works

Many of the theories of the state we have discussed so far assume that power is a zero-sum commodity – that the only way in which the powerless can gain power is to take it away from those who have it. Theorists in this school have also traced the different ways in which power can be manifested. Steven Lukes (2005), for example, identifies three dimensions of power. The first is where the powerful can directly dictate the actions of others; in the second, the powerful set the agenda or the terms on which issues are debated, what we might call the 'rules of the game'. The third describes how the powerless internalise and take for granted the assumptions of the powerful about what is and is not possible – power over ideas, akin to Gramsci's concept of hegemony.

A zero-sum analysis of power focuses on who has 'power over' whom and how that power is exercised. There are alternative approaches that analyse power as more fluid, as more diffuse and as something that can be generated and reproduced – as 'power to'. These approaches consider how power is produced and what it is that releases people's capabilities or power to act. Potentially, theorists in this school see power as a positive-sum game, although much of the analysis still focuses on the ways in which power and knowledge are manipulated in order to encourage the oppressed to see their interests as identical to those of the oppressor.

Much of this thinking draws on the work of Michel Foucault. His early writings explored the way in which mechanisms of knowledge and power shape or 'discipline' the 'subject', using increasingly sophisticated technologies of surveillance to create, classify and control society (Rabinow, 1984). Indeed, the burgeoning of online communication, electronic monitoring devices, smartphones and social media extends the potential for surveillance further than Foucault might ever have dreamt. However, while his analysis focuses on power as domination, Foucault's account does not see particular agents as possessing power – whether they be elites, classes or the state. Instead, he emphasises the 'capillary' nature of power and the way it operates through rather than on people. Central to his work is the argument that the exercise of power requires the compliance of 'willing subjects' and his exploration of how this compliance is secured. He emphasises in particular the significance of discourse as a vehicle through which knowledge and power are transmitted.

Foucault's ideas have been taken up by the 'governmentality' school, which explores the way in which governing has become detached from government and increasingly takes place 'at a distance from' the state. In this view, governing has become a domain of strategies, techniques and procedures through which different forces and groups in society attempt to render their programme operable (Rose and Miller, 1992). Governmentality theorists argue, for example, that through successive community programmes, local people are enrolled into governing themselves more effectively than the state ever could, 'acting as their own overseers, while believing themselves ... to be ... making their own choices ... and coming to their own conclusions' (Lukes, 2005, p 106). These programmes also make communities responsible for resolving problems which are often beyond their control – and easily blamed if they fail.

Bourdieu provides us with another lens through which to see the operation of power. His concept of habitus has been defined as 'the unconscious dispositions acquired through daily life' (Davies, 2011, p 63). It captures taken-for-granted patterns of thought, behaviour and taste that dispose agents to act and react in certain ways.

Individuals operate in a series of 'fields', each of which has its own dominant institutions, operating logics, means of production and ways of understanding value. They bring varying amounts of capital – economic, social and cultural – to these fields, depending on their background, education, wealth, networks and other attributes, and habitus structures the way they operate within them. This privileges certain actors over others and reinforces dominant power structures.

The understanding of power in these different conceptions can be taken to mean that domination is inevitable and agency an illusion. Indeed, Foucault's successors have often argued that, although the new emphasis on 'governance' rather than government suggests that governing is happening 'at a distance from the state', this is far from the case. The state, they argue, is furthering the neoliberal agenda, and its power continues to operate in these new governance spaces – much as Lukes' third face of power suggests.

This analysis – and particularly Foucault's emphasis on discourse – reflects Gramsci's view of civil society as the site where popular consent is engineered in societies, ensuring the cultural ascendancy of the ruling class and capitalism's stability. One example of the way discourse frames our world can be seen in the way that the language of the new managerialism gained ascendancy in the 1990s and continues to hold sway – for example, in the current emphasis on impact. Another can be found in the constant use by politicians of the term 'hardworking families', in contrast to the 'skivers' on benefits.

However, Gramsci, crucially, saw civil society as the arena where hegemonic ideas could be contested. In a similar vein, Foucault acknowledged that power could only be exercised over free subjects and therefore by its nature implies resistance: 'Just as discourses are diffused throughout society and power is everywhere, so too can resistance be encountered at every point, in attempts to evade, subvert or contest strategies of power' (Gaventa, 2003, p 2).

Translated into the current context, governmentality allows us to interpret neoliberalism not simply as an ideology or a political philosophy, but rather as an assemblage of techniques and technologies that facilitate the process of governing. This can then be interpreted negatively or positively. A negative view would trace the advance of the neo-liberal agenda through multiple capillaries and agencies, seeing its power as inevitable; a positive view would recognise the multiple sites through which power operates and thus the potential for change 'from below'. This opens the way not only for resistance but for the exercise of what Durose and Richardson (2015) call 'constitutive power', that is, forms of 'power with' that are co-produced, providing a synergy of experience and expertise.

Nor is Bourdieu's analysis as deterministic as it might sound. He acknowledged that at moments of crisis, critique and protest are possible because of the dissonance between subjective expectations and objective outcomes. However, Crossley (2003, p 49) goes further, describing how a history of contentious politics and the cultural capital it creates can create a radical habitus sustained by support networks, social events and pedagogic agents within a field, thus reproducing radical culture over time. The work of the Industrial Areas Foundation based on Saul Alinsky's ideas could be seen as an illustration of this.

For community development, these theories and ideas underline the need to understand how power works: to challenge dominant discourses and taken-for-granted assumptions: to make power visible and open to debate. It means that there are opportunities for communities to develop their own narratives and theories of change rather than allowing themselves to become complicit in those dictated by others. Communities can be encouraged to promote alternative agendas, to sustain a radical habitus through the activities and support structures Crossley describes or to develop constitutive power through forms of co-production as Durose and Richardson suggest.

Levels and dimensions of power

Empowerment has long been part of the language of community development and community policy, but it is a difficult and somewhat paradoxical concept. It can imply that power is being bestowed on communities (and by implication can be taken away again). The previous sections have discussed some different theories about who has power and how power works. Sherry Arnstein's (1969) famous ladder of participation addresses the question of how much power communities have. She suggests a spectrum of levels of influence from non-participation (manipulation and therapy), through degrees of tokenism (informing, consulting and placating) to degrees of citizen power (partnership, delegated power and citizen control). She argues, though, that many 'participation' exercises amount to little more than tokenism.

This ladder has been used many times to test out whether participation and 'empowerment' initiatives are giving communities real power over their services, economies and surroundings. It has been adapted and reworked but also criticised – for promoting a static view of power and assuming that community control is always the peak of achievement. Communities are not a homogeneous entity and Arnstein's analysis begs the question of how far those who are in control in the community are themselves sharing their power more widely.

A more complex model for assessing the way in which power is working in communities has been developed by the Institute for Development Studies. Their power cube (www.powercube.net) combines different aspects of power, equivalent to Lukes' dimensions described earlier in this chapter:

- The first is the form it takes, and this reflects some of the theories about how power works by differentiating between visible (observable decision-making mechanisms), hidden (shaping or influencing the policy agenda), and invisible (shaping norms and beliefs).
- The second relates to the levels at which it operates: household, local, national and global.
- The third differentiates between the different arenas in which power is acted out: 'closed spaces', where decisions are made by closed groups; 'invited spaces' where communities may be invited to join

with external actors but on their terms; and 'popular or claimed spaces', those that groups form for themselves, determining their own agendas and ways of operating.

They also extend the 'power over'/'power to' distinction to include power with (collective power, through organisation, solidarity and joint action) and power within (personal self-confidence, often linked to culture, religion or other aspects of identity, a form of power that influences the thoughts and actions that are seen to be legitimate).

The theories discussed here and the power frameworks with which the section finishes can help community development to understand how power operates and where the potential might exist to exercise agency and establish new 'circuits of power' (Clegg, 1989). They also address a central issue for community development – the question of 'structure' versus 'agency'. How far is the fate of disadvantaged communities determined by external factors? And how far can communities challenge dominant forms of power? The next section explores this question from an institutional perspective, asking how institutions frame the way that groups and organisations operate, or whether complexity theory offers a better understanding.

Organisations and institutions: how agency is organised

Many of the scholars we have mentioned are critical of the individualistic explanations of human behaviour that we explored earlier. For new institutionalists, organisational behaviour is structured by the fields in which people operate and the 'rules of the game' in those fields. These rules may be determined by a variety of forces – competition, the state or professions – and they structure the way organisations behave in three ways (DiMaggio and Powell, 1983):

■ Coercive pressures are imposed by resource providers or cultural expectations.

- Mimetic pressures lead organisations to copy other organisations that are seen to be successful, adopting 'best practice'.
- Normative pressures come from following professional or group norms and values.

These pressures are particularly strong in times of uncertainty – again, the rise of the new managerialism may be seen as a particularly powerful example, with managerial conditions sometimes imposed, sometimes copied in the hope that this will provide competitive advantage, or simply accepted as the norm – 'the way we do things now'. However, while communities need to recognise these pressures, they do not have to succumb to them. As Powell later acknowledged, there is scope for compromise or bargaining around government requirements and there are multiple sources of authority and guidance. Organisations may combine influences from dissimilar sources and pressures may be partial, inconsistent or short-lived. Community development can therefore help communities to question the 'rules of the game' by challenging assumptions, for example, about the way meetings should be run or how organisations should be structured. It can encourage groups to take their time to build relationships and trust, value informal processes, bring their own knowledge and experience to bear, and find alternative models to follow.

Systems and ecological approaches

The rational choice theories that have been dominant in policy tend to focus on individual self-interest and assume linear models of change, treating individual actors as if they operate in a vacuum. But some of the theories discussed so far argue the need for a holistic approach, understanding the behaviour of individuals, groups and organisations as part of a field or 'system' with independent and interacting parts. They also highlight the complicated dynamics of modern society. Systems models of thinking consider the whole set of organisations or stakeholders operating in a given situation and the way in which interactions between them influence each other's behaviour (Burns, 2007).

Complexity theory, for example, drawing on a variety of scientific fields, offers a much richer understanding of human behaviour than the rational choice theories of the economist. Complexity models of society emphasise the interconnectedness of life, suggesting that small-scale local interactions can result in major, unpredictable events (Capra, 1996). They tend to see social progress in terms of the evolution of new solutions or emergent forms of collective organisation, in ways that contrast with more linear explanations of change. Complexity thinking is used to explain two phenomena characteristic of communities operating as complex living systems: the emergence of familiar patterns and the occurrence of unplanned events (Gilchrist, 2009).

The implications of complexity theory for community development are that it is important to be alert to unplanned opportunities and to nurture connections by providing spaces and places for optimal levels of interaction. Helping people to develop networks and to allow new groupings to emerge from these relationships creates an environment that can enable change and sustain community activity. It also reminds us that there are many ways to view, interpret and shape the reality around us, and there are ambiguities and contradictions in any system that communities can navigate and exploit, even at neighbourhood level.

Social movement theory

We described earlier the distinction that the power cube makes between closed, invited and 'popular' or 'claimed' spaces. Social movements are perhaps the clearest manifestation of the claimed spaces that the power cube identifies – natural experiments in power, legitimation and democracy (Crossley, 2002, p 9). Social movement theory has borrowed from a range of disciplines to explore the political opportunities for change, the ways in which resources are mobilised and how issues are framed. All three elements have obvious relevance for community development.

One important factor in creating possibilities for challenge or change, according to social movement theory, is the political opportunity structure. Changes in elites and/or a transfer of power in government can prompt shifts in political alignments, with conflicts between elites, new access to decision makers and the potential for new alliances. They may introduce new institutional provisions for engagement and participation. Political openings are not, however, enough. The potential to exploit them will vary according to cultural and sociopolitical factors and opportunities may close again. So it is important to understand the factors that make for the successful mobilisation and organisation of resources.

At one end of the scale, social movement theory stresses the importance of networks in connecting people's personal understanding of their situation to collective action, as a way of making sense of their situation and sustaining a collective identity (Melucci, 1996; Castells, 2012). It highlights the importance of embedding a movement in existing networks, but also refers to the role of boundary-spanning connections in spreading its base beyond a narrow homogeneous core. At the other end of the scale, social movement theory highlights the function of social movement organisations (SMOs) as incubators of talent, collectors and disseminators of information, and springboards for mobilisation (Caniglia and Carmin, 2005).

SMOs and networks can help to keep movements alive during periods of repression or through ebbs and flows of interest. They allow people to stay in touch with one another, learn about new developments and mobilise should the need arise. But opportunity and mobilisation are not enough on their own to account for collective action. A third element of social movement theory relates to the importance of framing – the meanings and explanations that people bring to their situation (McAdam et al, 1996, p 5). As our earlier discussion of discourse and language implied, power can flow as much through meanings as resources. Movements based around feminism, disability equality, ethnic identity and sexual orientation have demonstrated this, challenging the predominantly male, white, able-bodied and heterosexual discourses that have framed reality and changing the way we use language.

Much has been written about the way in which traditional mass movements have given way to a new wave of social movements, organised around identity rather than class, that seek social and cultural transformation as well as political change (Melucci, 1988; Appiah, 2007). The internet and social media have further transformed the potential and organisation of social movements. Castells (2012) describes how these new technologies have given birth to new forms of organisation and politics supplementing and possibly supplanting the traditional political parties. These new forms, he argues, organise laterally through networks rather than hierarchically. We will return to the potential this opens up in Chapter Eight.

For community development, therefore, social movement theory highlights the importance of identifying and capitalising upon opportunities for change. It also stresses the value of framing issues in ways that expose and challenge dominant narratives but also capture the attention of both communities and policy makers. It validates the importance of organising through networks and finding the most effective balance between formal and informal ways of organising for change, opportunities that are enhanced by the new web-based technologies.

Brief conclusion

In Chapter Two, we introduced the idea of praxis: practical action based on informed discussion and reflection. If social change is to be achieved, there needs to be a continual interchange between theory and practice, with each learning from the other. But theorists develop their thinking within different schools and disciplines, and only too rarely do they enter into dialogue with one another. In this chapter we have introduced briefly some of the theories that can help us to think about how communities work, how they interact with the state and their wider environment, how power works and how change might be achieved. In the following chapter we will be looking at the way community development puts its values and ideas into practice.

Summary

- Theories of community generally differentiate between the organic communities associated with the past and the more functional identity-based communities associated with contemporary society.
- Social capital theory suggests that social bonds and connections are as important to the health of society and democracy as other forms of capital. Bridging and linking social capital are both needed if social change is to be achieved but they can sometimes be in tension.
- Psychological theories help us to understand group development and dynamics. They also explore how people make sense of the situations they find themselves in, how they learn and the choices they make.
- Theories of self- and collective efficacy emphasise the importance of social context and collective experience. The structural factors that affect communities often undermine efficacy, but community workers can play a role in generating more positive experiences and rebuilding confidence.
- Theories of the state can be differentiated between those that see state and community in opposition, and pluralist models in which the state mediates between different interests. The former underpins a radical model of community development; the latter suggests a role as broker helping groups to negotiate the system.
- Theories of power can be based on a zero- or positive-sum model. The former tends to emphasise structure, but the latter suggests the potential for agency. The power cube developed by the Institute for Development Studies (www.powercube.net) can help groups to explore different dimensions of power.
- Theorists show how power can be hidden and how discourse shapes our perceptions of our world. Community development has an important role in exposing hidden assumptions and drawing out alternative ways of understanding experience.
- Institutional theory explains the pressures on groups and communities to conform, but in a complex society the interactions between different stakeholders can lead to new forms of organising.

■ Community development can look to social movement theory to suggest how to identify and maximise opportunities for social change.

Further reading

A short guide can only give readers a brief introduction to the different theoretical approaches that can inform community development and readers are strongly advised to explore the wider literature on the ideas that particularly interest them. There are also important groups of theory that we have not been able to touch on here, in particular, feminist theory and other theories concerned with equalities and discrimination. Keith Popple's *Analysing community work* (2015) includes a useful analysis of these theories and critiques.

David Halpern's books on social capital (2005 and 2009) set out the benefits to society of common values and associations, while Ben Fine (2001) provides a useful critique of social capital theory.

Stephen Lukes' *Power: A radical view* (2005) is an excellent and accessible guide to different theories of power. The power cube, along with a much fuller discussion of its evolution and ideas, can be found online: www.powercube.net. Those who are prepared to engage with more academic prose will find a thorough discussion of governmentality in Peter Miller and Nikolas Rose's book *Governing the present* (2009), particularly the chapter 'The death of the social', and the section within it called 'The birth of the community'. Jonathan Davies (2011) also provides a valuable critique of governance theory from a Gramscian perspective. All these texts cover the work of Foucault, but readers can also find an introduction to Foucault's own writing in Rabinow's *The Foucault reader* (1984). Sidney Tarrow's classic study of social movements (2011) provides a brilliant overview, as well as ideas on repertoire that community development workers can apply in practice.

Writing specifically for community development readers, Margaret Ledwith (2011) provides an excellent introduction to Gramsci and Freire, as does Keith Popple (2015). Peter Somerville's (2011) *Understanding community* explores social capital and Bourdieu's habitus in some detail, while Catherine Durose and Liz Richardson (2015) provide a valuable analysis of positive (constitutive) and zero-sum (constituted) power in policy making. On the web, reviews of community and social capital at infed (the encyclopaedia of informal reading – www.infed.org) are well worth reading.

The present authors have also explored these ideas further. Alison Gilchrist's *The well-connected community* (2009) shows how ideas of networking can be used by the community development worker, while much of the theory on power introduced in this chapter is discussed in more detail in Marilyn Taylor's *Public policy in the community* (2011).

5.

effective and ethical community development: what's needed?

As we saw in Chapter Two, community development is fundamentally concerned with helping communities to help themselves and to achieve greater influence over decisions that affect their lives. This chapter will look at the methods, resources and attitudes that help communities to develop a sense of their own rights and responsibilities, and their capacity to achieve change. It reminds us that important principles underpin community development and considers what is needed to support effective practice, including the skills and techniques that characterise this (see FCDL, 2015). In doing so, it will address long-standing debates over whether community development is best seen as a set of practices, an occupation, a profession, an intervention or a movement.

Community development has many components (see Box 5.1). First among these are the unpaid efforts and expertise of members of the community – so-called 'ordinary' residents who take on roles as leaders, volunteers, committee members and so on to set up, run and participate in a whole variety of community-based activities. Working alongside them, especially in the most deprived areas, might be professionally qualified community development workers, who have demonstrated their competence and understanding, often at graduate level. These could be employed by the local authority, a voluntary organisation, a public health body, a partnership or even the community itself, perhaps under the auspices of a tenant-owned housing co-op or residents' association. The last survey of community development workers carried out in the UK found that approximately half were employed in the voluntary sector, with slightly under that proportion based with statutory bodies, mainly local councils but also some healthcare trusts (Sender et al, 2010). Although posts have been drastically reduced following spending cuts, the ratio is likely to be the same, though possibly with an increase in positions created through national bodies, such as Locality or Local Trust, and reaching into target communities on a less intensive basis.

Box 5.1 IACD's Guiding Principles for Community Development

1. **Local Leadership**: The community plays the leadership role in its own development.
2. **Government Supporting Role**: Government actively facilitates and supports community development through the provision of information, expertise, guidance and other resources, as appropriate.
3. **Collaborative Approach**: Community development builds on co-operation, co-ordination and collaboration between communities, government and the private sector.
4. **Sustainable Balance**: Community development builds on a balanced approach that addresses and integrates economic, social, environmental and cultural considerations.
5. **Respect for Local Values**: Community values are understood and respected.
6. **Diversity, Equality and Social Inclusion**: All community members, regardless of gender, age, ability, race, culture, language, sexual orientation, or social and economic status are empowered and engaged in the community development process and are able to access its social and economic benefits.
7. **Transparency and Accountability**: Community development encourages transparency, accountability, participation and evidence-based decision making.
8. **Partnerships and Shared Interests**: Community development engages the necessary partners in the community and from government.

9.   **Common Vision**: Community members work together to define a common vision for the future.
10. **Focus on Community Assets**: Community development is built on existing community capacity and assets.
11. **Volunteerism**: Community development values, respects, nurtures and encourages volunteerism.

Source: http://www.iacdglobal.org/about/vision

As we have already noted, not everyone who works with communities can be described as a community development worker. However, people in other roles and disciplines may perform aspects of community development even though the words do not appear in their job titles. These include frontline staff delivering public services such as, for example, police officers, street cleaners, park keepers, housing officials, health visitors or school caretakers. The way they do these jobs can encourage people to share responsibility for their environment, raising issues of concern and working in partnership to create solutions that work for local people. If so, then they could be said to be part of a broad, usually unco-ordinated team which is working to empower communities and develop better relations between the state and the public. In recognition of the value of working in partnership with communities and the voluntary sector, many local councils and larger housing associations employ community engagement or tenant participation officers who have lead responsibility for strategies to improve dialogue and co-operation between agencies and residents. Backroom staff, such as planners, service managers and communications units, can also play a role in making sure that information is available to the public in friendly and timely ways, and that the views of communities are taken on board wherever feasible.

Effective community development needs competent practitioners with access to necessary resources and support, and operating within a broadly defined set of principles and processes. In addition to generic skills and values that can be applied in any role or setting, the community development worker must have a good understanding of the context: the local specifics and relevant policies and funding opportunities. However, as we saw in the introductory chapter, community development is generally considered to have a value base that promotes the common good, challenges injustices and nurtures individual and collective growth. In real life situations this is often more complicated than it sounds, and some of the associated dilemmas and challenges are considered in greater depth in Chapter Seven.

Working with people in groups

Community development work involves working directly with all sorts of people in all sorts of roles. Therefore, good 'people skills' are essential to engaging with communities and helping people to work together. Community development workers must be active observers and listeners, empathising with what they see and hear, and establishing a rapport with a wide range of people. Being able to build relationships easily and to develop trust and mutual confidence requires a good sense of self and a willingness to 'act naturally' in different settings. Community development workers need to understand the diversity of cultures and abilities in the communities they are working with, and must be sensitive to differences as well as being aware of inequalities and strains between different groups. They will encourage individuals to take on roles or tasks that will stretch them a little and to question prejudices or behaviours that are oppressive. As we shall explore further in Chapter Seven, this may involve dealing with negative emotions such as fear, resentment, anger and hurt, in addition to challenging damaging and discriminatory attitudes.

Mostly, community development work is about encouraging people to think creatively and collaboratively so that they are able to devise solutions to shared issues, develop community leadership and resolve conflicts. This requires skills in persuasion, negotiation and informal coaching, usually on a one-to-one basis but occasionally as part of the support given to a group. Group work may involve being able to facilitate discussions, help members to co-operate, overcome difficulties, and mediate tensions and conflicts. Meetings are an important aspect of community development, providing a forum where communities can share experiences, debate how they would like to see things change and take decisions about what needs to be done. The worker often plays a role in setting up the meetings, publicising and servicing them, and may even chair them, at least in the initial stages. Meetings should normally be as inclusive as possible and encourage maximum participation, so knowing when and where to hold them, as well as how to set agendas, arrange the furniture layout in the room, take minutes, prepare posters or communicate through social media are all useful skills.

However, a great deal of community development takes place outside formal meetings, through informal conversations, chance encounters and spontaneous activities. Ideally, meetings of community members should be as informal as possible, making sure that people feel comfortable and that their contributions will be heard and valued. Too much emphasis on formal rules and regulations can stifle discussion and preserve existing power roles, so it is a good idea to make sure gatherings of community members are inclusive, friendly and fun. Sharing food together is a great basis for people to get to know one another, and icebreaker games can help to overcome initial shyness or suspicion so that relationships within the network grow stronger and group dynamics settle down to a working 'norm'.

Dealing with difficulties

An important role for practitioners is to maintain an overview of the community's interests, networks and potential for change, so that they can work with people to respond positively to changing circumstances and not necessarily defend the status quo. Encouraging community members to 'let go' of cherished ideas that no longer work and enabling new forms of collaboration to emerge can be a really valuable contribution to the development of a community, especially if lessons are learnt and shared along the way. It is therefore crucial to focus on collective benefits and community goals rather than the specific needs and desires of individuals, however articulate, angry or assertive they might be. Particular skills are needed in knowing how and when to challenge people constructively so that unhelpful attitudes and personal antipathies do not hold back progress, discourage participation or prevent people from learning from one another.

Community development workers are often on hand to help groups and organisations that run into difficulties, perhaps due to an undemocratic or burnt-out leadership, failure to attract new members, personality clashes, ideological disagreements or diverging interests. These problems might reflect internal tensions or changing circumstances. They may require mediation, a rethink of an organisation's priorities or a deeper cultural change to allow alternative agendas to emerge. Facilitating these discussions, advising on transitions and dealing with the inevitable fall-out are important aspects of the community development role which demand high levels of skill and understanding.

Working with organisations

As we saw in Chapter Two, organisational development is a core aspect of community development and there may come a point, usually as a group expands or becomes more ambitious, when it may choose to turn itself into a more formal organisation. This is neither inevitable nor necessary, and the best course of action might be for a group to remain relatively informal and channel formal procedures (such as employment or financial accounting) through an already constituted body. Nevertheless, 'incorporating' a group so that it becomes a legal entity in its own right has the advantage of limiting the liability of individual members and trustees because the organisation as such is able to enter into contracts, such as leases for premises, or to employ staff. If things go wrong despite the board or committee acting reasonably and with 'due diligence', then the individual decision makers are protected from being held responsible, as only the corporate organisation can be sued. The community development worker should therefore be in a position to advise the group on the different forms that incorporation might take and whether it is wise to register as a charity. In the UK there are a number of options to consider regarding legal incorporation, including becoming a charitable incorporated organisation (CIO), a community interest company (CIC), a community land trust, or a community benefit society (BenCom, formerly known as industrial and provident societies). These options allow different modes of operating, with or without charitable status, and require different governing documents. It may be advisable to seek legal advice before deciding on format, as this can help groups to consider what they want to do and which legal structures are appropriate to their current aims.

Box 5.2 Growing and changing an organisation for older people

Some retired people began to meet regularly to enjoy doing things together such as day trips to local places of interest. A community worker helped them to set up a bank account, apply to a charitable trust to cover some of the costs of transport and suggested that they open up the group to others in the community. They were happy to do this and discovered that many older residents were lonely and needed day-to-day contact to help with household chores and maintenance tasks. The group set up a home visiting service and gradually raised a grant to provide a subsidised 'handyperson'.

In order to safeguard the funds and employ someone in the role of handyperson, the community worker worked with a small committee to establish the group as a community benefit company, which later registered for charitable status. As new members came on board, some of the current officers found it difficult to accept the changes needed, but the community worker was able to handle these discussions and allow the original founders to bow out gracefully, while encouraging the others to take on responsibility for running the organisation.

There are numerous guides available from the relevant national infrastructure organisations to help choose the right format and think through the transition between different stages (e.g. Rochester, 1999; McMorland and Erakovich, 2013). One obvious gain from incorporation is that the organisation is normally in a better position to attract external resources and credibility. A formal structure also offers a decision-making framework for accountability and management that may help the organisation to be more stable and sustainable. The worker may assist the group with devising its internal governance procedures (such as explaining officer roles and collective responsibilities, elections or sub-groups) and she or he is also likely to support the organisation with its external relations, perhaps through a newsletter or social media, to encourage ongoing community engagement and transparency. This is important because organisations that don't refresh their membership, maintain their profile and evolve with changing circumstances can become moribund or close altogether. On occasion, the best course of action will be to assist an organisation to end, either by merging with another, closing down or going into temporary hibernation. Knowing how to help an organisation 'shut up shop' in a graceful way has real value in terms of acknowledging, indeed celebrating, the group's achievements, tying up loose financial and administrative ends, and leaving a lasting footprint in the community.

Networking and engagement

Community groups and voluntary organisations rarely operate on their own. They form part of a rich ecology sometimes known as the 'third sector'. In areas where this is thriving, there will be strong networks that connect individuals with common interests. The community development worker can encourage networking by organising activities that bring people together to share resources, combine efforts and build campaigning alliances.

Successful organisations evolve (not necessarily by formalising their structures) and can be helped to do this through developing wider links, which give access to information about the bigger policy or financial context in which they operate. Community development workers are often to be found setting up and servicing multi-agency networks, which bring together people who have overlapping goals but wish to retain their autonomy. Being involved in these types of bodies allows groups to share their ideas with like-minded people and to work collaboratively around common issues. By acting together, communities develop a stronger voice and greater negotiating power with other bodies, but, conversely, they may need additional support to ensure that their views are heard among the professionals in multi-agency coalitions.

It is thus important to consider the wider picture, including the availability of bridging and linking social capital. Community workers need to be aware of the constellation of groups, partnerships and organisations that make up the local community and voluntary sector. Sometimes the most effective course of action may be to forge links with other bodies that can challenge or overcome a particular blockage or come together to seize an opportunity that is too big for a group to deal with on its own.

Alongside the direct work of supporting communities to organise independently around issues that they define as priorities, community development workers play an important role at the interface between communities and statutory or private sector bodies that want to work with local people or relevant voluntary organisations. Sometimes this is about providing forums where council officers or other professionals can meet with residents to debate how services can best be provided locally. At another level, the worker may support the development of partnership working, liaising between sectors to ensure that those involved understand what contribution they can make and easing some of the inevitable tensions that arise due to clashes in organisational cultures or competing interests. The worker may need good brokering, mediating and interpreting skills when working across such boundaries, and will often find themselves translating official jargon into language that community members can relate to. From their usual position on the periphery or outside large institutions, community workers often have a good overview of how the separate functions operate in the community and find themselves helping colleagues to join up across departments in a more co-ordinated approach.

Working across organisational and sectoral boundaries has been shown to be a key, but not always recognised feature of community development practice (Gilchrist, 2009). Workers based in the statutory sector – for example, working for a police authority or public health body – have a crucial role in maintaining relations with communities, particularly the most disaffected or marginalised. Community development can provide a strong and sustainable foundation for co-production and citizen empowerment by creating the conditions and capacity for more equal dialogue and co-operation. It enables authorities to understand and work with communities better, challenging their somewhat bureaucratic processes and introducing different forms of communication and engagement that encourage more diverse and democratic participation.

Box 5.3 A model for empowerment practice

Ketso is a toolkit first developed in southern Africa to help communities be involved in planning village improvements. It consists of a portable set of branches and leaves made out of material that can be written on and stuck to panels to encourage reflection, discussion and decision making. It encourages creative problem solving and has been successfully used by communities to plan how to develop a sustainable strategy for food production and sales in Swaziland, to explore budget cuts relating to Portsmouth Harbour and to set up a social enterprise for a network of creative artists. It is said to boost confidence and hope, while making sure that people share information and ideas with relevant stakeholders.

Source: www.ketso.com

Community workers employed by statutory agencies play an important role in challenging taken-for-granted cultures within their own organisations, and can work with colleagues to change structures and procedures that exclude or inhibit community engagement. Within communities, community development creates a wider pool of 'active citizens' who have the confidence, skills and knowledge to act as community leaders or representatives. The network of groups, forums and organisations operating at community level can ensure that these people are supported in their roles and held accountable for their decisions. Thus, community development is a vital ingredient in strategies for increasing the influence and responsibility of communities over the design and delivery of public services, either directly or through involvement in cross-sectoral partnerships.

Getting to know the community

The skills discussed so far are general capabilities in which any community development worker employed in any setting should feel competent. In addition, the worker will need to develop knowledge and understanding of specific communities and their circumstances if she or he is to support their activities and promote effective development. Community development must start from 'where people are at now', not where we think they should be. This is known as a 'bottom-up' approach and contrasts with a more 'top-down' model whereby the agenda is set externally by national targets, area programmes or funders' priorities.

Community development workers need a good understanding of the area in which they are based: the key players, organisations, networks, current pressures and future aspirations. It is useful to know something about the history and customs of communities living in the area, as well as their hopes for the future. Do people from different backgrounds mix or are there antagonisms that tend to keep some community members apart on a day-to-day basis? Other factors to investigate might be patterns of migration, living standards and health. How does the local economy function and how has it changed in recent years? What about transport connections and the reputation of the area among outsiders? What facilities does the locality enjoy? What is lacking? Are there plans for its regeneration or other improvement strategies being developed by the authorities? And perhaps most importantly, how are things experienced by community members: what do they want to see changed and what do they want to preserve?

Simply walking about an area, having one-to-one conversations and door-knocking are good ways to contact and talk with the individuals who are not so prominent in community networks. They may care passionately about where they live and have interesting ideas about what could be improved. This features as a core method in the community organisers model. It can be fairly intense and time-consuming, but offers a way of reaching residents who are not already involved in the various local groups and activities. Crucially, it requires the worker to be able to glean information from informal observations and encounters, and to understand the meaning within conversations, stories and traditions. This information can also be conveyed non-verbally, though body language, street sounds, graffiti or the appearance of buildings; so workers can develop a well-rounded picture of what's going on in a community, that isn't just based on what they are told, either informally or officially.

The asset-based approach (see Chapter Two) emphasises the need to discover and build on community strengths. It is useful to undertake some kind of audit of assets to create a positive profile of what skills, talents, expertise, traditions and physical resources are available (Packham, 2000). This can be achieved through involving community members in participatory action research or a systematic community audit to draw up their own community profile or investigate a particular issue (Hawtin and Percy-Smith, 2007; Mayo et al, 2013). There are lots of creative ways of gathering evidence and ideas using film, video boxes, systematic observation, reading relevant official reports and perusing local media, including any online websites. Many villages and neighbourhoods host online community forums where local information, debates and announcements can be found. Related Facebook pages often carry dialogue about community issues and it may be worth looking at the websites of voluntary organisations that serve different communities living in the area.

In order to work effectively with a community, the worker needs a sound and up-to-date cognitive map of the physical and psychological geography of an area, the significance of different boundaries and the usage of important community facilities. It is useful to understand how residents behave in spaces and places at different times of the day, for example, the flow of children and parents around school gates, the queues at the post office, the gatherings outside the mosque for Friday prayers or attendance at regular sporting and cultural events.

Community development workers should know how to access relevant information about the communities they are working with from formal sources such as the media, census figures, surveys or data on levels of deprivation. This may involve being able to interpret and apply the findings from recent research or consultation exercises. Information and statistics about official indicators of 'deprivation' covering employment (and unemployment) rates, health levels, housing conditions and demographic patterns can be obtained from council websites and are broken down into small areas. Care should be taken in how this information is construed to avoid false generalisations and labelling communities as disadvantaged. Nonetheless, the kinds of problems that a community profile reveals often match the issues that communities themselves want to address. As we will see in the next chapter, politicians and policy makers in national and local government are also concerned with improving health, education, housing, integration and so on.

Resources and support

Political rhetoric sometimes seems to imply that communities can deliver services for nothing by mobilising unpaid labour through volunteers and activists. This is based on a partial knowledge of the community and voluntary sector and is misguided. Social action and volunteering are generally enhanced and more sustainable if people have access to professional support, often in the form of community development practitioners. Communities also need money to run their activities, albeit on a small scale. They often struggle to raise funds, through jumble sales, raffles, sponsored events or membership dues. These may cover basic running costs but do not allow for growth and innovation.

Community development workers play a key role in helping groups to obtain the resources they need to achieve their goals. Usually this is some kind of funding, which might be used to buy staff or equipment, and may result in the acquisition of a building or other facilities, such as a minibus or an all-weather sports court. The competences associated with resources include all aspects of fundraising: knowledge of potential sources for grants and donations, being able to work with communities to draw up a budget and put together an application for funding, and a rudimentary grasp of financial accounting to make sure that money is properly spent and recorded.

Even quite small grants for community development can make an enormous difference, such as seed corn funding for a new initiative, to lease some vital equipment, to arrange an exchange visit or to hire a meeting room. Ideally, these should be readily available and without strings attached, perhaps at the discretion of a local councillor or community development worker. Some areas have experimented with communities having control of a budget that is ring-fenced for community benefit. These models are known as community chests, local social capital or participatory budgeting. Decisions on the allocation of funds are made at open meetings at which members of the public or community representatives listen to the applicants and agree where the money can best be allocated. Such exercises are themselves forms of community development because they are empowering, they build links across communities, raise awareness and encourage a variety of skills, including presentation, advocacy and negotiation. They may, however, need careful preparation and facilitation to make sure that the procedures are transparent and fair.

Access to or, better still, control of some kind of communal building can make a huge difference. This could be as basic as a community room in a block of flats, right through to a purpose-built centre with offices, performance space, sports facilities, a cafe and training rooms. Current policy on the transfer of assets from local authorities to community ownership (see Chapter Three), can make vital resources available for community use, but can also leave communities straining to maintain them unless they receive some level of financial or community development support.

As we saw in earlier chapters, a key purpose of community development is to shift the distribution of power and resources in society, especially for disadvantaged communities. Workers should therefore know how to attract (and manage) funding for community projects and prepare basic business plans for the takeover of assets. Perhaps more importantly, they should be able to share this knowledge and these skills with community members so as not to encourage over-dependency (of which more later). This could be through formal training workshops or informal buddying or shadowing schemes for willing residents who want to take on these roles. This is sometimes known as capacity building, and involves developing people's confidence as well as specific skills and knowledge among community members.

Neither community development workers nor residents need to know everything about all of these matters, but they should know how to access external advice and expertise, for example, from infrastructure support organisations, such as local councils for voluntary service (CVSs). (Contact details for local CVSs can be found through the NAVCA website – see Appendix.) These provide specialist services to the third sector and formal training in committee skills, leadership, governance and fundraising.

Supporting opportunities to learn

When getting involved in running community activities, some people find they need to develop new skills and knowledge, for example, in order to arrange effective and democratic meetings, to take minutes, to organise events or services and so on. They may want or require training in financial accounting; health, safety and hygiene regulations; protection procedures for children and vulnerable adults; all aspects of computing; staff recruitment and supervision; equalities policy and practice; or any number of topics which are unfamiliar or where existing knowledge needs updating. Adult and community education courses, especially where these are set up in response to community requests, can greatly enhance people's confidence and their ability to carry out roles within the community. The learning gained from experience, discussion and observation is also valuable and, as we saw in Chapter Two, community development workers play their part in supporting informal education.

One of the roles of community development practitioners is therefore to encourage and draw out learning from experience so that community members become individually and collectively more confident and more powerful. Transformational approaches argue that community development must move from change at community level, scaling up interventions by connecting to social movements and national consortia.

Community development emphasises the value of experiential learning, with many people starting their career as community activists and volunteers. For people who are new to community development there are taster sessions or standalone workshops offering an introduction to community development or a chance to develop skills in group work, fundraising, running meetings or similar techniques. These are complemented by short courses that may be relevant to particular applications for community development, such as health, social investment, equalities and so on. There are a range of recognised qualifications in community development, many based on the National Occupational Standards. Drawing on Freire's 1972 model of social pedagogy, community workers see themselves as trainers and educators, albeit usually through informal means, and they should have skills in running workshops, supporting action learning and facilitating dialogue, as well as knowing how to question and learn in order to improve their own practice.

Working with volunteers and activists

Volunteers are an essential part of the resource base for community action and being able to support and co-ordinate their efforts is a vital aspect of the community development role. The term 'volunteer' is used here to include anyone who has made a free choice to be involved in a community group or activity and is not being paid for their contribution (though they may receive out-of-pocket expenses). Individuals are motivated by many different interests and emotions, and these may change as people get more confident and involved, perhaps moving into roles with greater responsibility (Ockenden and Hutin, 2008; Rochester, 2013). A volunteer could therefore be a parent or childminder helping to run the local toddlers group. The committee members of the estate tenants' group are volunteers, as are the community representatives on the crime reduction partnership board. After-school clubs and youth centres may have trained and paid workers but are often assisted by a team of dedicated volunteers, all of whom have to be vetted and supervised. Community activists are also volunteers, often putting in long hours in pursuit of their passion or campaigns.

People who are active in their own communities and in pursuit of their own collective goals do not necessarily see themselves as 'volunteers' in the traditional sense and they may have an uneasy relationship with paid community workers. Some community activists lack confidence. Others can display dogmatic arrogance or single-minded devotion to their 'cause'. It requires great skill and diplomacy to find out how individual members of the community can most effectively contribute towards achieving shared goals and be rewarded for their efforts. While they are to some extent free agents, there are inevitably expectations (and some regulations) that govern their involvement, especially where the welfare of children or vulnerable adults is concerned. Helping volunteers to make full use of their talents, to surprise themselves, to learn from each other and to work as part of a team is essential to community development. Volunteers come from all walks of life. They may range from high performing mavericks, used to getting their own way, through to dedicated leaders and followers, including individuals with low self-esteem and possible mental health issues. As well as offering much-needed time and skills, they often bring emotional demands and discriminatory attitudes. All this needs careful handling and clarity. Such difficulties can be compounded when the worker is line-managed by a member (often the chair) of a voluntary management committee.

Working with members of the community who are volunteering their time and energy is a normal facet of community development. This gives rise to a number of dilemmas that aren't generally encountered when dealing with paid staff with clear job descriptions and positions in the hierarchy.

Although community development workers may be employed in the voluntary sector, the focus for their work is usually at the level of the community sector: the smaller, less formal groups and networks that have fewer resources and are often run almost exclusively through voluntary effort (Richardson, 2008; McCabe et al, 2009). The existence of these groups seems to be more precarious and less visible to outsiders, and their potential can be overlooked in favour of the more stable and accessible voluntary organisations that may have a local presence but are not always run by local people.

Communication and knowledge management

Keeping track of all this information can be challenging to say the least, requiring either an excellent memory or, more likely, good record keeping. Concerns about the ownership of information gathered by and about communities have been broached in relation to data protection and the role of paid staff. There are also more fundamental issues about status and respect for 'local' knowledge and residents' rights to determine how their area is described. Community development workers should consider carefully how information is communicated among colleagues, whether through the informal grapevine of gossip and rumour, or in official directories or reports.

Information technology has developed rapidly in recent years, allowing sophisticated databases to be devised and interrogated containing up-to-date knowledge of communities and their environments. Web 2.0 software has created a whole new dimension of community development, with local neighbourhood websites, blogs and chat forums providing platforms for inter- and intra-community communication. Evidence suggests that these enable people to engage with local decision-making and collective initiatives even if they are at first reluctant to come to public meetings or become involved in face-to-face interactions (Burrows et al, 2005). Presentation and media skills are vital for communities to counter myths and negative images. Community workers can work with local people to challenge these discourses and to offer alternative 'narratives' that change public awareness and understanding. In Chapter Eight, we flag up future possibilities for the use of new communication technologies and note that current political trends are towards much greater transparency in sharing information between government bodies and communities.

Community development workers are often themselves trusted sources of information. They have a responsibility to share what they know (unless there are grounds for confidentiality) and to enable communities to develop their own means of communication. This means understanding the dynamics of local communication systems: the mechanisms and conventions for sharing ideas and knowledge, the way information flows through a community and the mechanisms by which communities can articulate their views to leaders, representatives and decision makers. However, communities rarely speak with one 'voice' and community development workers need to be confident in facilitating discussion, managing dissent and mediating conflicts.

Encouraging dialogue and debate is a crucial aspect of the role, and this can take considerable skill, especially when feelings are running high. There are, however, a range of tools and techniques available that can help meetings to reach consensus or to set priorities.

Using and influencing policies

Communities are part of larger social, economic and political systems, and community development workers need to be able to operate within these but also attempt to change them if necessary. They should have some political acumen, understand the policy making process and know how to be effective on committees and working groups. Having a sound understanding of the wider context and systemic pressures will make them more effective as negotiators and, on occasion, able to oppose the abuse of power or information.

An effective community development worker therefore needs to be aware of the current policy environment, including any pertinent legal rights and responsibilities, and, perhaps most importantly, any opportunities for political leverage for gaining resources, such as through asset transfer, service contracts or programme funding. This requires a good knowledge of local decision-making structures: local authority committees as well as any forums and panels where communities can talk with their elected councillors and officers. There may also be cross-sectoral partnerships and consortiums operating to deliver services while community engagement exercises will pop up from time to time. An important role for the worker is to make sure that community members are able to influence these or become valued partners. Careful judgement and debate is required in deciding whether taking up such options will be worthwhile or simply divert energy and time from community efforts to achieve more meaningful change.

A good community worker will also be alert to opportunities to exert influence and obtain resources, perhaps by exploiting uncertainties or divisions between decision makers, or by finding allies in unexpected places. As Chapter Four suggests, there is much to be learnt from the experience of social movement activists, especially in relation to levering open 'cracks' in the system and mobilising people around a common cause. The practice of community development is also potentially affected by a plethora of policies and organisational procedures, some of which may be contradictory.

Box 5.4 Understanding policy tools

A tenant participation officer for a large housing association was able to use the organisation's policies on antisocial behaviour and equalities to ensure that residents experiencing homophobic harassment were protected, while the perpetrators were moved to a different estate with both support and sanctions in place to encourage them to change their attitudes. A thorough knowledge of the relevant procedures meant that the victims' privacy was respected and they gained much-needed security in their own home. The association's commitment to equality for all tenants led to a mini-poster campaign in the area, which in turn generated a great deal of discussion.

Competencies and core values

Over the years, there have been several attempts to define the skills and knowledge required by competent community development workers. The latest of these are the national occupational standards (NOS), developed by the Federation for Community Development Learning (FCDL) following widespread consultation in the field – a full description can be downloaded from www.fcdl.org.uk. They are broadly accepted by practitioners, trainers and employers, and used to write job descriptions and person specifications. Occupational standards are also being used across a number of workforces (for example, in Wales) to manage performance, deliver training courses and identify staff development needs.

Practitioners are encouraged to reflect on their work, focusing on the how and why of what they do, as well as specific results. As we have already said, community development is a values-based approach that is informed by an enduring set of principles. These are:

■ social justice
■ equality
■ participation

- empowerment
- collective action
- co-operation
- learning.

Just how these principles are put into practice will be determined by local conditions, community priorities and external factors such as funding criteria and policy goals. Nevertheless, they provide an ethical framework that will guide how a worker behaves as well as how their performance will be judged by members of the community and their managers.

Whatever course of action they take, whichever objectives are chosen, community development practitioners need to embed these values into their decision making and interventions. Until this becomes automatic, it is helpful to have some kind of mental checklist or set of guiding questions. For example, they may consider the following:

- How should a meeting be organised so that most people can attend and are able to contribute to the proceedings?
- How can the people affected by a decision be involved in influencing what happens?
- What obstacles are preventing people from working together and how can they be overcome?
- Do community members have equal access to resources and opportunities?
- What can be done to challenge prejudices and power imbalances between different sections of the community?

As well as upholding these core values, community development workers depend on their personal principles and characteristics. They must understand how to make 'use of self' in their role as an employee, but also acknowledging their social identity as members of different communities, possibly including as a local resident. Regardless of circumstances, effective and ethical workers will be continuously reflecting on their own motivation, judgements and practice, ideally with the help of some kind of supervision or mentoring. Informal discussions with peers also help people to explore how different facets of their lives are relevant to their work, and what biases these might entail.

Brief conclusion

Community development takes time, commitment, resources, practical skills, self-awareness and a huge amount of trust. It does not offer a quick fix to society's problems; rather, it is an approach to working with communities that builds relationships, acknowledges people's contributions and capabilities, and aims to address shared problems through collective solutions. In this regard, it has similarities with modern social movements but has a clear commitment to enabling communities themselves to set the direction and pace of change.

The competence model that emphasises occupational skills and knowledge appears to focus on the 'job' aspects of community development while its concern with standards suggests an orientation towards professionalisation that not everyone will agree with. Community development requires more than a set of skills, resources and competences, being based on principles, processes and beliefs that ensure that communities are empowered, that individuals are encouraged and that groups are enabled to achieve their own ends to the benefit of others across the wider society.

Summary

- Community development takes place in many different settings but is shaped by a set of agreed principles.
- It can be generalist or specialist, and delivered intensively, with a 'light touch' or at 'arm's length'.
- Many people working with or in communities use community development practices to improve community engagement and services.

■ It primarily involves helping people to work together in networks, groups and organisations, and often involves nurturing connections across community and sectoral boundaries.

■ In order to work from the 'bottom up' it is necessary to know how specific communities work and how community members view their situation and prospects.

■ Helping communities to acquire and manage funds and assets provides vital resources for further development.

■ Community development supports people to learn skills, build and share knowledge, and to become more confident in their capacity, as volunteers and activists, to run things for themselves or to push for improvements.

■ Local knowledge is an important resource for community development and should be properly managed and shared through effective communication channels.

■ Community development sees itself as operating within political systems. It shapes and is shaped by policies and power relations.

■ There are recognised national occupational standards that set out agreed core values and competences need to perform the community development role.

■ Community development can also be seen as a broad approach akin to a locally rooted movement for social justice.

Further reading

Henderson and Thomas's book on *Neighbourhood work* remains a classic now in its fourth edition (2013), while Alan Twelvetree's latest version of *Community work* will be published in 2017.

The *Community development challenge report* (CLG, 2006) provides a useful overview of practice and some challenges. The national occupational standards (NOS) have recently been revised and set out the different roles and skills required for effective community development. They are also available in Welsh. A summary framework is available from FCDL.

There are also numerous guides on community development and engagement in different settings. Many were published by the Community Development Foundation, some of which are now available from the British Library directly as hard copies or to download (via http://socialwelfare.bl.uk/). Useful guides are also available from the Scottish Community Development Centre.

6

applying community development in different service areas

Community development can contribute to outcomes in many different policy fields: cohesion and integration, community safety and crime reduction, culture and the arts, education, environment and sustainable development, health and wellbeing, housing, and local economic development among them. Much of the early community development in the 1960s and 1970s focused on housing, leisure and play, for example, since these were the issues raised by residents in the public housing estates where many community workers were based. Community development workers supported campaigns for housing improvement and rehabilitation, and helped to form and provide support for residents' associations. They also supported residents in campaigning for play and leisure facilities and running playgroups and community centres. In subsequent years they have supported tenants in taking on the management and even ownership of housing, and most recently supported campaigns to improve conditions for private tenants, to resist evictions and to campaign against benefit cuts that force families to move hundreds of miles away from their communities.

Box 6.1 Action on housing

ACORN International (the Association of Community Organizations for Reform Now) was set up in the US in 1970 and now works in some 17 countries. The UK's first branch and head office was established in Bristol in 2014 by two graduates from the UK Community Organisers Programme with a colleague, and there are now five branches across England, with a sixth due to be launched. ACORN UK describes itself as 'building a union and movement of low-income communities, organised and united for social change'. An early success for the Bristol branch in 2015 was the adoption of an ethical lettings policy by the City Council, achieved with the council's first ever unanimous vote. It is now working to extend endorsements of the charter across landlords, lettings agents and charities. It has also supported individual Bristol tenants, preventing evictions and rent rises and securing much needed repairs.

Source: www.acorncommunities.org.uk

By building 'bridging social capital', community development also plays an important role in fostering community cohesion. It can help 'new' communities to settle, providing information and advice about local services, for example, or guidance on their entitlements and responsibilities. It can also help them to form their own associations and support groups, and to be involved in wider initiatives such as local festivals or forums. Conversely, by providing advice and 'myth-busting' information, and promoting cultural awareness, community development gives 'host' communities a better understanding of the newcomers and helps them to welcome new communities more readily. People who are confident in their collective or cultural identities are more likely to engage with others beyond their community. Community development can support both incoming and 'host' communities to develop this confidence.

Box 6.2 Sowing the seeds of solidarity

The Comfrey Project in Newcastle runs allotment sessions for refugees and asylum seekers, providing a safe and welcoming environment. As well as enabling the members to grow their own food, attendance has improved their English and increased levels of interaction with other allotment users. There is a shared lunch and members are encouraged to join other community activities in their areas. They are also referred to other agencies if they need specialist advice or support. Their confidence has increased and prejudice against refugees has also been reduced as local people become aware of the situation of the refugees and asylum seekers and hear the true stories of why they had to leave their home countries.

Source: www.comfreyproject.org.uk

Fear of crime and community safety are other issues that concern both policy makers and local communities. Community development has worked with the victims of crime to set up support groups and to organise campaigns that highlight particular kinds of assault and harassment, such as those based around hate and prejudice, drug dealing or antisocial behaviour. Community development approaches have also been used by public authorities and voluntary organisations to improve community safety, for example, in relation to arson, traffic accidents and domestic violence. These have often involved public and peer education about risks, but there has also been a commitment to listening to community concerns, developing solutions that will work in given circumstances and generally trying to improve relations between community members and public services, such as the police, fire fighters and planners.

Fear of crime is a real issue in many disadvantaged communities. On the one hand, it makes people unwilling to engage; on the other, it can be whipped up in ways that result in vigilante campaigns – against paedophilia or drug dealing for example. By developing informal social networks and strategies to report milder forms of vandalism or dangerous and antisocial behaviour, community development can increase people's sense of local pride and mutual responsibility, break down barriers between residents, and between residents and institutions, and give them the confidence to address more serious issues.

Community development can also help to address the educational underachievement that characterises many poorer neighbourhoods. It can build links between schools or colleges and their communities, which give communities access to new resources. Community development can involve parents in their children's education – parents who might be reluctant to engage in a system that has failed them in their own past. It can also provide informal education opportunities. This may give people the confidence to return to formal learning, but it also demonstrates the value of alternative approaches to education, which validate and expand people's existing knowledge, and help them to build the skills and assurance to engage as citizens on their own terms. Mayo and Annette (2010), for example, document the story of a government initiative – Take Part – that used informal education to encourage active citizenship.

Box 6.3 Community learning and education for change

The workers' education movement has a long history in different parts of the global North, from the Workers' Educational Association in the UK to the Danish Folk High Schools. It has continued to underpin community development approaches to emancipatory education. Another influence has been the development of leadership programmes for social change in the communities that suffered most from the injustices of society, through organisations like the Highlander Research and Education Center in Tennessee and the Industrial Areas Foundation in Chicago (founded in 1932 and 1940 respectively). Both traditions emphasise learning through action to promote change. This approach also lives on through a number of international capacity building agencies – such as Civic Driven Change in the Netherlands and Participatory Research in Asia (PRIA), based in India – as well as in trade union initiatives and work with tenants of social housing – for example, the National Communities Resource Centre at Trafford Hall in England.

In these and other policy areas, community development workers support communities in campaigning for better services, in negotiating with private and statutory providers and in running their own services.

They help communities to access the information and other resources they need and to demystify professional interventions. They also work with professionals to help them understand and respond to community needs.

In the rest of this section, we focus more closely on the contribution community development can make in four particular policy fields. The first three are very much at the forefront of current policy: environmental action, economic development and poverty reduction, and health and wellbeing. The fourth demonstrates the contribution that arts and cultural activities can make to community development and community cohesion. In each case, we set the policy context, ask what community development can offer and highlight some of the challenges that the policy field poses for community development.

Environmental action and sustainable development

Context

Over the past few decades, there has been a growing realisation that climate change really matters and that humans have a responsibility to share and protect the environment for the sake of future generations and biodiversity. The earth's resources are limited and are not being used fairly or sustainably. Policy goals in many parts of the world acknowledge that people have a right to live in a decent, clean and healthy environment. The organisation Living Space Project (formerly Capacity Global) explains environmental justice as being based on notions of social justice and equality, with an added slant towards green issues (see www.livingspaceproject.com). Nowadays there is more awareness of the impact of global warming and the need to reduce our 'carbon footprint'. There are many claimants to the origin of the slogan, 'Think globally, act locally', including the community organiser Saul Alinsky. But whoever first coined the phrase, it is clear that communities, government and individuals need to take action to safeguard the environment and ensure that future economies are sustainable.

Across the world growing concern about climate change is generating enthusiasm for local measures that reduce greenhouse gas emissions and lessen our dependency on fossil fuels. Community-level resilience strategies, using local knowledge and solutions, help to mitigate the effects of global warming, such as flash floods, heatwaves and extreme weather patterns, by developing practical measures for coping with, and then adapting to, these increasingly frequent events. As well as defending communities from their immediate impact and dealing with the aftermath, community development can build organising capacity and collective solidarity.

An EU-wide target has been set to generate 15% of our energy needs from renewable sources by 2020 and the Paris 2015 agreement has committed all governments to reducing carbon emissions. Policy in the UK encourages voluntary and community organisations to develop their own initiatives and to be involved in local planning to address this challenge. There are a growing number of community groups seeking to reduce their carbon emissions and generate energy from renewable sources, for example, through hydroelectric schemes harnessing the power of local rivers. Renew Wales, an independent body that advises communities, has supported a huge range of enterprising projects, including local food production, nature conservation, recycling and awareness raising (see www.renewwales.org.uk).

In Scotland the land reform movement has provided new opportunities for communities to buy land and use it for local benefit, notably the creation of wind farms that can produce a significant income to invest in local projects. The Centre for Sustainable Energy offers useful guidance to communities in England wanting to do more in their own neighbourhoods (see www.cse.org.uk), suggesting a myriad of possible initiatives, from wholesale neighbourhood planning or district heating schemes to more piecemeal projects around waste recovery, alternative modes of transport, or the preservation of green spaces such as a local woodlands or parks, which can provide a haven for wildlife as well as opportunities for outdoor play.

In some cases, communities have worked with local authorities to develop larger-scale schemes around transport and housing, for example, to build sustainable apartment blocks or create safe routes to schools to encourage children to walk or cycle rather than being dropped off in cars by their parents. These initiatives make it easier for people to protect the environment and reduce energy consumption within their normal everyday lives.

Box 6.4 Sustainable living

In Tipperary, Ireland, the community of Cloughjordan has acquired a 68-acre plot of land in the centre of the village and is aiming to build 150 houses using sustainable construction materials and techniques, such as solar panels and a shared heating system. This eco-village is managed by the residents themselves and includes allotments and a community farm that supplies food for local consumption. The village as a whole is committed to using permaculture and fashioning a car-free environment, with a newly established bicycle shop thriving as more and more residents are persuaded to leave their cars at home.

(See www.thevillage.ie for more information.)

As well as contributing to the 'green agenda', community-led environmental projects may have additional outcomes, for example, economic benefits through the creation of jobs for residents and developing local supply chains and outlets for food. 'Green volunteering' and outdoor activities boost both physical and mental health, as does the presence of trees and the chance to spend time in natural surroundings. Biodiversity can only flourish if *all* ecologies are nurtured and respected.

What can community development offer?

There are many ways in which community development supports environmental action and a number of 'clean and green' initiatives have been promoted by government and local authorities. Community 'clean-ups' and 'litter picks' can be organised at very local levels (for example, by the parish council) or they can form part of national campaigns to 'keep Britain tidy'. Increasingly, communities are reclaiming abandoned sites for public use, creating community gardens or space for growing food. 'Guerrilla gardening', as it has become known, has gathered momentum, inspired by the Incredible Edible initiatives in Todmorden in northern England (Warhurst and Dobson, 2014).

Under the 'community rights' agenda, communities are being encouraged to take on responsibility for local assets and services and, as a result, there are rising numbers of 'friends of ...' groups. These are replacing council maintenance teams with volunteers managing local environmental resources that form the 'green infrastructure', such as commons, parks, village greens and canals. Communities are often concerned about threats to their area from pollution, traffic congestion, developments on cherished open spaces (for example, from proposals for housing developments or fracking) or the arrival of a superstore displacing shops that sell local products. Community development helps community members to organise around these issues, mobilising protestors and ensuring that counter-arguments are well presented and persuasive. Assisting communities to organise local 'walkabouts' or 'open homes' enables people to identify opportunities for environmental improvement and to learn from households that are already trying to live sustainably.

Community development can also put people in touch with what's happening elsewhere, for example, arranging visits to places where local communities or 'transition towns' have set up projects, sometimes as social enterprises. These might be funded initially through community shares, or run in partnership with private companies, for example, wind turbines that feed electricity into the national grid thereby producing a financial return on the investment.

Box 6.5 The community benefits of renewable energy

When plans were announced to build a wind farm in the local area, Fintry Development Trust (FDT) took the opportunity to negotiate the addition of one community-owned wind turbine. It has since carried out energy surveys of each house in the village and is in the process of providing insulation for each surveyed home. It has also made village amenities more energy efficient by installing a new heating system in the village hall and a biomass heating system in the local sports centre. It has recently funded improvements at the local school and started a car-sharing scheme as well as a growing project and community orchard.

As well as promoting sustainable development, FDT aims to provide employment for local people, provide affordable housing to young people and develop the skills of people in the village.

Adapted from Aiken et al (2011)

Recycling schemes can be especially effective, both creating income from waste management contracts and also enabling people to swap, share and trade the resources that are surplus to their personal requirements. Websites such as Freecycle (www.freecycle.org) or web-based neighbourhood tool share schemes (see for example www.streetbank.com/splash?locale=en) can help to tackle poverty, foster community connections and reduce demand on landfill sites (Seyfang, 2009).

Box 6.6 Food production in an urban setting

Sustainable agriculture does not just have to take place in the rural countryside; there are many examples of city farms around the UK. In Dalston, East London, a disused shop has been converted by the community to provide ingenious growing spaces, including an indoor allotment, micro-fish farming, and a rooftop chicken coop and polytunnel. This hyper-locally produced fresh food is available through a cafe on the premises and a community market.

(For further information visit www.farmlondon.weebly.com.)

Challenges

Disempowered people living in degraded streets or barren rural areas may find it difficult to accept some responsibility for a global threat. For many people experiencing poverty and discrimination, the environment might not seem a major priority, even though pollution, traffic, diminishing resources and rising costs of energy hit the poor hardest, and they usually have fewer means of escape or protection. We have witnessed how environmental disasters such as hurricanes, flooding, mudslides and forest fires have wiped out homes and livelihoods for subsistence populations in developing countries. Environmental justice applies equally to communities the world over.

Communities will only be motivated to protect their environment if they think that they have some stake in it at a local or personal level. The challenge is to find an issue that people not only feel they have in common, but also one where they believe that their actions can make a difference.

Attempts to combat climate change through community-level schemes may meet with scepticism and local resistance due, paradoxically, to their impact on the landscape or disagreements about how community benefit funds might be invested. Nesta's Big Green Challenge programme found that community enterprises clashed with the business culture of private sector firms, causing tensions and mutual suspicion (Cox et al, 2010). All these difficulties may block progress until a consensus can be found and it requires diplomatic leadership and skilled application of community development principles to overcome the obstacles and negotiate a way forward.

Economic responses to poverty and social exclusion

Context

In the UK we are witnessing widening inequalities (Dorling, 2015) and growing absolute poverty (Clark, 2014) along with the increasing stigmatisation of the poor. Despite the discourse of 'hardworking families' that we referred to earlier, the restructuring of the labour market around low paid, insecure jobs means that many of these families are themselves in poverty and reliant on benefits and tax credits. Meanwhile, any income they do have 'leaks out' of the neighbourhood to external businesses, energy providers, landlords and loan sharks. Many of these areas have been abandoned by services, local retailers and financial institutions (Sherraden and Ninacs, 2014, pp 18–19) and this isolation from the mainstream often prevents them from taking advantage of economic resources and opportunities.

One of the costs of industrial and economic change – as the CDPs noted 40 years ago (CDP, 1977) – has been that regions created by industry have been deserted by the industries on which they depended, leaving many areas without jobs and the skills necessary to compete in today's economy. Housing policy over the years has led to the concentration of poor households in social housing, with high levels of unemployment in specific estates and inner-city neighbourhoods. In response, the regeneration programmes described in Chapter Three have taken a comprehensive approach designed to tackle not only lack of income and employment in these areas but the ill-health, educational disadvantage, insecurity and environmental degradation that are often part of the spiral of disadvantage they represent.

In addition to these broad, holistic programmes, more targeted initiatives include those aiming to:

- **increase income** – through improving access to jobs and training, enhancing working conditions and job security, increasing benefit take-up, promoting community enterprise, social investment and, potentially, through asset transfer and contracts for local services

- **reduce expenditure** – through debt advice, energy saving schemes, community transport and local food production
- **share and redistribute resources** – through co-operative housing, credit unions, LETS (local exchange trading schemes), Timebanks, bulk-buying and recycling projects, and community shares.

Government support has recently focused on supporting communities in building the capacity to take on assets and services. But, as we saw in Chapter Three, there is a risk that smaller organisations will lose out on contracts because they cannot compete with larger voluntary and private organisations. The trend for payment by results places an emphasis on demonstrating impact, which is especially difficult for smaller organisations dealing with the most marginalised users.

There is a growing emphasis on social investment in current national programmes across the UK, including those funded by the Big Lottery Fund. Big Society Capital is a major new source of support through community finance intermediaries. And there has been a huge growth in the community finance sector over recent years: the value of lending capital held by Community Development Finance Institutions (CDFIs) increased by 22% between 2006/07 and 2007/08 (GHK, 2010) and by 2013 CDFIs served 52% more customers than in 2012 (CDFA, 2014).

What can community development offer?

Many of the initiatives listed above, especially those to reduce expenditure and keep money circulating locally, have come from communities themselves. The previous section has described some of the local food production and energy initiatives, for example, while community enterprise and asset development has a particularly strong tradition in Scotland, Wales and Northern Ireland.

Community development can work with communities to identify opportunities, develop ideas, and scope potential markets and likely investors. Community organisations may need support in developing the skills and knowledge required to run a business, and community development can build confidence as well as developing an array of relationships that will support individuals, organisations and groups. It can signpost them to external resources, such as technical expertise, financial advice or information to help them assess and manage the risks involved in running a business, including taking on paid staff. And it can put them in touch with other groups who have valuable experience to share. Community development can also work with communities to ensure that schemes remain inclusive and accountable to the wider community, that they are fair and transparent in their dealings, and that they empower community members to contribute to decision making about the direction of work.

Challenges

There is considerable concern about the pressure from government to transfer responsibility for services – and the associated risks – to community enterprises. Critics argue that this will simply add to the pressures on poorer communities and that social finance products will serve government and market priorities rather than those defined by communities. Aiken et al (2011) point out, for example, that many community organisations running buildings do not want to expand, preferring simply to act as stewards of an important local resource. Assets easily become liabilities when buildings fall into disrepair and community members can overextend themselves in taking on new responsibilities. The demands of running an enterprise can separate social entrepreneurs from their community roots and it is important that new community enterprises do not unbalance existing informal networks and support organisations within the community.

The potential for growth in the social enterprise sector remains to be seen. Recent research by the Institute for Public Policy Research (IPPR) (Cox and Schmuecker, 2010) indicates that many enterprises continue to rely on grants several years into their existence, and there is a high failure rate. Despite the rhetoric about citizens running services, the current legal and policy framework in the UK is ambivalent towards community ownership, while mainstream financial institutions remain reluctant to lend to small locally owned enterprises. However, Murtagh and Goggin (2015) counsel against a rejection of the possibilities of social investment, arguing that it is necessary to work with the economic system and its structures in order to challenge it (in the same way, perhaps, as community development practitioners have written about working in and against the state). They argue that social investment can 'liberate as much as it can discipline', by giving an example of a technical aid organisation in Belfast which has been able to challenge elite regeneration projects and protect the designation of social housing sites through using social finance to reduce its dependence on government.

Box 6.7 The potential of social investment

Community Places in Belfast is a technical aid organisation that advocates for neighbourhood groups in disadvantaged areas across Northern Ireland on housing, planning and regeneration issues. It has negotiated a loan to help it establish a new planning advice centre to strengthen service provision and reduce its dependence on government funding. It has also established a separate trading arm to strengthen earned income, deliver contracts (including government) and carry out research. This has allowed it to 'do [its] own thing with local groups', including a major campaign to resist the re-zoning of social housing.

Adapted from Murtagh and Goggin (2015)

There are also examples in the UK and beyond of ways in which community development can adapt state agendas in line with their own agendas and values.

Box 6.8 Learning from international practice

A resident-led organisation in Luton – Marsh Farm Outreach (MFO) – is testing out the Organisation Workshop model developed by Clodomir Santos de Morais in Brazil. This is a 'learning-by-doing' approach, noted for enabling the creation of jobs and social enterprises by and for unemployed people. Working with the local Jobcentre Plus, MFO have developed an intensive training programme for 40-plus unemployed people to build up their organisational and technical skills through the development of local enterprises, which address locally identified problems and bring resources and skills back into productive use.

(See www.marshfarmoutreach.org.uk)

It is important to recognise that many communities have made conscious choices to run their own services, feeling they can offer something the state cannot provide (Richardson, 2008). But, even so, encouraging community enterprise is about more than offering start-up grants and business advice; it needs to be part of a wider empowerment process and to open up possibilities for new economic models rather than necessarily fitting into those imposed from outside. International models, like the Grameen Bank founded in Bangladesh, have attracted widespread interest and there is a strong social economy tradition in Europe. But in the UK and US the policy emphasis has been on business performance and capacity to earn income as opposed to social innovation and ethical outcomes, let alone finding new solutions to the challenges that communities face (Defourney and Nyssens, 2012; Murtagh and Goggin, 2015).

Health and wellbeing

Context

Community development has long been seen as a means of addressing problems around health and social care, and it is one of the few areas where community development continues to enjoy both interest and funding, especially in Scotland. It has been used by community and public health practitioners and has also found favour with policy makers as a way of involving patients and the wider public in making decisions about health services. More recently, the co-production model has attracted attention as a means of sharing responsibility for the wellbeing of individuals and communities between professionals, patients and ordinary (or perhaps lay) members of the public. Community development has much to offer here through supporting self-help groups or schemes such as 'good neighbours'.

The government is interested in person- and community-centred approaches and in increasing 'health literacy' across the general population so that people are better able to navigate the health system. This should help people to access and understand information and advice about their health needs and treatments (see, for example, www.knowledge.scot.nhs.uk/healthliteracy.aspx).

Complicated, chronic health problems are associated with low incomes, poor housing and stress, so a collaborative approach is needed that tackles the causes not just the symptoms of poor health. This requires a multi-agency approach (Orme et al, 2007) and in England responsibility for public health strategies has been returned to local authorities to be overseen by boards that involve partners from different series, including voluntary organisations and community-based self-help groups. Similar arrangements are in place in the other jurisdictions, with community health partnerships (or their equivalents) aiming to improve wellbeing and better integrate heath and care provision.

Community engagement has a growing evidence base as a method of improving community health, alongside volunteering and expert patient models (NICE, 2008; Mundle et al, 2012; O'Mara-Eves et al, 2013). Communities that have limited access to opportunities for exercise and who live in impoverished environments experience higher than average rates of heart and respiratory disease, sometimes exacerbated by obesity and stress. This holds true across many countries and is attributed to, amongst other things, the pressures of living in an unfair economic system where rewards and opportunities are unevenly distributed with little prospect of change (Wilkinson and Pickett, 2009). Unsurprisingly, there is a disturbing correlation between poverty, poor health and early death, creating what Marmot calls a 'social health gradient' (2010, 2015). There is also evidence that suggests that people's level of social capital – the strength and diversity of their informal networks – affects individual resistance to infection, contributes to speed of recovery and generally supports a sense of mental wellbeing (Halpern, 2005; Christakis and Fowler, 2009).

In Western societies there are growing concerns around obesity, the ageing population and mental health problems, especially for young people. Increasing demand is placed on over-stretched health provision, with high expectations for expensive treatments and emergency care. Spending cuts mean that clinical resources have to be prudently rationed. It is no wonder, therefore, that policy makers are interested in ways of harnessing community ideas and energy to promote better health and find alternatives ways of caring for people who are ill, frail or temporarily incapacitated. These include volunteer schemes, peer education, social prescribing, public participation exercises, co-production models and strengthening community relationships.

What can community development offer?

By taking an empowering approach to health, community development can contribute to all of these policy aims through helping communities to tackle some of the causes of ill-health and create opportunities for living healthier (and happier) lives. Simply bolstering community networks, building capacity and reducing the social isolation caused by ill-health can improve wellbeing. One approach to improving social care, for example, has focused on strengthening community capital and neighbourliness (Knapp et al, 2013; Parsfield et al 2015).

Community development enables community-led health organisations to work in partnership with public sector bodies, and it can work directly with marginalised communities to develop skills and confidence that allow local assets of all kinds to be applied to improving health outcomes. Community development has a long tradition of helping people to campaign against local conditions that give rise to disease and reduce life expectancy. For example, tenants' organisations have taken up housing issues such as dampness, pest infestations and expensive heating arrangements.

Individuals with particular interests, conditions and expertise may seek to be more involved in determining local priorities in health provision or to improve how services are delivered and taken up, especially in situations where some sections of the population appear to be disadvantaged or neglected entirely. Ensuring effective community engagement between patients and service users and health decision makers is an important role for community development, but communities can also be supported to develop their own self-help activities to address what they believe are the causes of poor health. For example, communities who are concerned about the limited options available to buy cheap and nutritious food have set up their own schemes for growing, selling and cooking local produce (see Box 6.6). Conversely, some communities have challenged the dominance of outlets for cheap alcohol and fast food on the high street, arguing that these make it too tempting for people to opt for the easy choices that are bad for health.

There is currently a lot of interest in asset-based, co-production models of health provision using integrated strategies, such as Healthy Living Centres or Recovery Colleges. These offer holistic approaches to mental health and wellbeing that are accessible and relevant because they involve communities in managing the facilities and deciding on how preventative measures, care and treatment can be made available to suit local preferences (Foot, 2012). Providing opportunities for exercise, volunteering and social interaction encourages people to make links with others in the community and share responsibility to make sure that people receive the care and support they need. There are many opportunities for communities to co-operate with health agencies to promote healthy choices or improve access to health services through outreach, peer education and patient participation groups.

Box 6.9 Peer-supported public health

In Newcastle, HealthWORKS has a track record of training and employing local people to work with communities as link workers or health trainers. They use asset-based, community development methods to help residents tackle the problems that they identify for themselves. Describing their approach as 'support from next door not advice from on high', they provide an empathetic and confidential ear, signpost people to suitable local activities and offer follow-up support along the way. In some cases, the workers have helped residents to establish and support community groups and networked across the area to co-ordinate the different organisations.

Adapted from www.healthworksnewcastle.org.uk, with thanks to Barbara Cage

Challenges

Illness and infirmities are often regarded as an individual, private or 'lifestyle' matter and therefore addressed through attempts to change everyday behaviour or to improve people's access to health and care provision. Health professionals trained in the medical model tend to focus on diagnosis, treatment and prevention at this level rather than listening to community views on how residents would like to see things improving or trying to address neighbourhood harms or even socialeconomic issues such as income inequalities. Community health programmes are therefore usually top-down and follow externally set agendas. As we have seen, community development takes a different approach, getting alongside and empowering people to identify and tackle the things that they collectively rank as most damaging to their wellbeing. This mismatch between models, professional mindsets and organisational cultures has sometimes made it difficult for the health system to make use of community development, even though it recognises in principle that supplementary community-based approaches are needed for effective prevention and compliance strategies (South et al, 2015). The Healthy Communities: Meeting the

Shared Challenge programme in Scotland worked with local planning partnerships to promote a good understanding of the contribution that communities can make to tackling health inequalities and improving wellbeing. This national capacity building programme proved effective in helping to share good practice and find ways of 'scaling up' initiatives that seemed effective. Finding a shared commitment and appropriate language is crucial in enabling community development to make meaningful inroads, especially during periods of tightly constrained budgets and where there is a strong emphasis on outcomes.

People's assessment of their own health is affected by a range of factors: some in the external situation, others in their personal experience and psychology. It can be useful to take a systems approach, working simultaneously to understand the interaction between different life experiences, shared social conditions and agency responsibilities. The C2 model adopts a multi-agency approach, emphasising 'connecting communities' and 'building partnerships', and encouraging professionals to pay close attention to community needs and aspirations. C2 has been pioneered in practice by former health visitor Hazel Stuteley and her colleagues, and is loosely linked to HELP (the Health Empowerment Leverage Project) which was commissioned by the Department of Health to demonstrate cost-effective strategies for community health (Stuteley and Parish, 2010).

Despite the complexity of this approach, it seems to be successful, although it faces some of the same difficulties as community development generally in robustly attributing outcomes to specific interventions.

Community crafts, arts and culture

Context

The terms 'art' and 'culture' are often associated with wealth, power and the elite. But they also offer a route through which many people engage in local community and public life. For many under authoritarian rule, arts and cultural activities have been the only means of expressing and maintaining solidarity, as the folk societies in Hungary and elsewhere in Central and Eastern Europe demonstrated during the Soviet era. Art also provides more overt symbols of resistance – it is usually the songs and images of a campaign or social movement that live on in people's minds.

In recent years there has also been a movement to re-evaluate craft activities (such as knitting, metal work, lace-making and so on) for their contribution to the health and social wellbeing of individuals and whole communities. Crafts organisations can create a democratic space for participants to discuss matters of personal or local concern – quilting, for example, has provided opportunities for local debate as well as making a strong democratic statement to the outside world. Age UK's Men in Sheds projects have been shown to improve their members' mental health as well as enabling them to produce artefacts for community use, such as benches or bird boxes.

Many of the benefits of arts, craft and cultural activities may be individual: research suggests that they build confidence and self-esteem as well as giving people opportunities to learn new skills. They give people a voice and are powerful tools for learning. There are also collective benefits, however. These activities can forge a community identity and generate community pride. They provide opportunities for people to socialise and work together. They allow marginalised communities to be seen and heard in the outside world, changing the image of an area and bringing outsiders into areas they wouldn't normally visit – virtually or in real time. By providing safe spaces for engagement and expression, they can increase understanding and bridge ethnic and generational divides, for example, through the exchange of skills and designs.

Arts and culture can also be a potent instrument of social change. Their immediate appeal reaches people that other kinds of intervention cannot reach. They can involve people in many different ways. Art crosses boundaries. Globalisation has brought the people's art into homes across the world, whether it be folk music, graffiti or the artefacts of traditional cultures.

What can community development offer?

With its social justice goals, community development works to ensure that the arts are democratic, inclusive and socially engaged. It provides opportunities for people to have their own creative voice but also to make connections and work collectively. In this sense, the process is as important as the product. The community development literature provides many different examples of this, from the very simple expedient of taking visual minutes at meetings to involving residents in major multimedia events.

Community festivals and carnivals are powerful expressions of community identity and offer opportunities for the expression and celebration of diverse cultures. They contain various elements, involving local people as individuals, schools and clubs in performance, costume and exhibition design, and building parade floats, as well as simply offering a space for people to come together.

Community theatre has been used to tell the history of an area, involving large parts of the community – again often through schools and local associations. It may be used to explore and re-enact local histories, to engage different parts of the community in discussion about issues of local concern or to highlight these issues to the wider community and external actors. Alternatively, local venues may set up outreach projects to reach people in nearby public housing estates who would not normally go near a theatre. In the global South, participatory forum theatre is used to galvanise community action and for education purposes (Boal, 2008).

Box 6.10 Pictures of health

The New Vic Theatre in Newcastle-under-Lyme hosts a community project, Borderlines, that uses cultural animation techniques to work with local people and draw out their ideas on a variety of topics that are affecting community lives, such as bullying, knife crime and 'honour violence'. It facilitates creative activities, through drama and craft materials, to encourage participants to share their 'untold stories' and aspirations for the future.

In a recent collaboration with Keele University and Kindle public health consultancy, groups worked together to fashion 'pictures of health' that conveyed important ambitions about how people imagined good health. Another project used role play and storytelling to reveal aspects of volunteering that caused both pride and concern.

(See www.newvictheatre.org.uk/new-vic-borderlines-2)

There are many examples in the literature of young people engaging through music and video production, through setting up local radio stations or through the use of the internet and social media. This gives them skills, brings their voices into a wide arena and challenges stereotypes.

Local home-grown and web-based media also challenge the hegemony of the globalised media and corporate branding and help to cement local identity. With suitable community development support, community or 'free' radio has also nurtured community relations by creating the means by which incoming refugee and migrant communities organise to articulate their issues and ambitions, while simultaneously building links with other local groups. For example, in Austria, community radio has become an important vehicle for community cohesion and capacity building, providing opportunities for volunteers to learn language and technical skills, as well as providing platforms to debate local issues.

Box 6.11 How art brings reconciliation and recognition

Valentina Baú (2015) describes how participatory video has acted as a peace-building tool for young people in the Rift Valley in Kenya. While thinking back to past events in order to tell their stories was painful, the video gave the young people and their experiences recognition in the wider community and a sense of agency, as well as opening up dialogue between tribes.

Murals can brighten up a neighbourhood and reinforce community identity. Graffiti walls engage young people and may turn a problem into a solution. Children in one estate designed the new security gates that were needed, turning a negative into a positive asset. As a study of murals in Ireland has demonstrated, 'Simply planning, executing and enjoying these activities can counteract the exclusion of local residents from local urban decision making processes' (Grant-Smith and Matthews, 2015, p 150).

Finally, museums might work with the local community to bring local history projects to life. Local history has also been a focus of writing projects and some community centres employ a writer or artist in residence to work with local people.

Challenges

Community arts work is versatile. In terms of the outcomes that policy makers are looking for, it can tick a lot of boxes, contributing to educational achievement and physical improvements, and sometimes bringing jobs into the community. But developing community arts can be a tough call. A special issue of the *Community Development Journal* in , October 2007 (volume 42, issue 4) warns that the globalised media can have a devastating effect on traditional forms of culture and practice. It also underlines the tendency for art and cultural activity to bolster dominant ideologies. And it is important to avoid treating community arts activities as remedial, or expressing patronising attitudes towards anything that is produced.

The literature also highlights the dangers of commodification and exploitation. There are obvious ironies in the fact that graffiti – the art of the ghetto – is now the subject of glossy coffee table books rather than challenging the consumer economy.

Arts and craft ventures may have a lot of impact in the short term, but they may offer a panacea rather than addressing the root causes of social problems. They need to be part of a longer-term strategy creating opportunities for dialogue, debate and exploration if they are to serve longer-term community development goals. And while they may get people involved, they are prey to the pitfalls of any other kind of community development: graffiti – for example in conflict zones – may be divisive and threatening instead of inclusive.

A successful arts enterprise may not touch large parts of the community. Artists can be solitary creatures and persuading them to work in a collegial way – where the ideas come from local communities rather than from the artist – can be difficult. There is also a huge culture clash between the artistic world and the managerialism required of funded community work projects.

Finally, in times when resources are scarce, there is a demand from funders for robust evaluation. The impact of arts work is as hard to measure as any other form of community development. But some funders are turning to art itself as a way of evaluating and communicating what community ventures are achieving. Local Trust has commissioned a longitudinal multimedia evaluation to present learning and progress in fifteen Big Local areas over time through film, photography and audio. This will engage local residents themselves in using film and photography for self-evaluation.

Brief conclusion

The sections in this chapter demonstrate that community development – as a broad-based approach that starts from people's own concerns – can contribute to many different policy areas, supporting community participation and generating community solutions. But because it is a generic practice, it is not confined to particular policy areas. Food and energy projects, for example, can have health, environmental and economic benefits for a community.

Summary

- Community development contributes to effective working in a range of policy areas.
- It enables professionals to identify and respond to community priorities in services and planning.
- Community development enhances participation, especially in relation to those groups that are more difficult to engage.
- But community development poses challenges in relation to decision making, which policy makers and service providers are not always equipped to handle.
- It is essential that communities are able to play to their strengths and not expected to take on responsibilities regardless of their capacity to do so.

Further reading

Each of the policy areas described here has its own specialist literature:

- Project Dirt is a UK network of people and projects using social media to connect like-minded people who are working on environmental issues. From their website you can learn more about a wide range of community-level activities: www.projectdirt.com. Localise West Midlands has published a report on mainstreaming community economic development (Morris et al, 2013) and the New

Economics Foundation (NEF) is always a good source of information on the most recent ideas and innovations: www.neweconomics.org.

■ For additional community development materials on health and wellbeing, visit the CHEX website: www.chex.org.uk.

■ The *Community Development Journal* has produced a special issue on community development and the arts (volume 42, issue 4, October 2007). The journal also contains many articles in its general issues addressing the topics discussed here (see, for example, Kim, 2016; Lesniewski and Canon, 2016; Sievers, 2016 on employment and labour market issues).

Some of the textbooks on community development mentioned elsewhere in the Short Guide have chapters addressing the contribution community development can make to specific issues (see Somerville, 2011, for example).

7

challenges for practice

Throughout this Guide we have identified a number of challenges for community development. There are intrinsic tensions within community development practice to which there are no easy answers, although individual workers may well find pragmatic solutions that reflect local conditions, priorities and relationships.

While many believe that the methods and values of community development make it indispensable, practitioners experience a number of tensions and dilemmas that arise because of their role and commitments. The situations they find themselves in are rarely straightforward; in fact, they are often characterised by ambiguity, sometimes generating conflicting loyalties and 'role strain' (Hoggett et al, 2009). As a form of intervention, community development operates at different levels and is located in a wide range of agencies, including trade unions, faith-based organisations, even some local campaigns run by political parties. Within local authorities, for example, it may find itself spread across different departments: sometimes at the heart of the hierarchy, more often on the edges or within specialist teams. Its purpose is still contested and it is frequently carried out through short-term projects, fragmented funding and precarious job contracts making it difficult to carve out a strategic and sustainable approach.

Developing a strategic approach

Community development has suffered in the past from being relatively unstrategic, at a national level and also at district or sub-regional levels.

The *Community development challenge* report, commissioned by the Department for Communities and Local Government and published in 2006, attempted to address this in its analysis of the state of community development (see Table 2.1). It made a series of recommendations regarding the status of the occupation and the evidence base as well as the need to be more strategic (CLG, 2006).

We have already noted that community development is a long-term process. It is most effective when it forms part of a coherent strategy that sets out the various steps or objectives that will be undertaken to make progress towards goals of social justice, community empowerment, better local democracy or whatever policy has highlighted.

For community development to become more strategic, at least two aspects need to be considered. First, how can community practice be better mainstreamed – that is, understood and embedded within services and organisations that engage with the public on a statutory basis? Second, how can the core of specialist community development workers be better supported and more effective? Unfortunately, most of the national infrastructure and membership networks that have brought practitioners and activists together and acted as champions for community development in the past have either already shut up shop or are in danger of doing so due to loss of core funding. Others have become more dependent on government contracts, making it more difficult for them to exercise an independent critical role.

Although community development has no statutory basis in the UK, a study of the experience of developing community development strategies for local authority areas has highlighted a number of benefits (Community Development Exchange, 2008). A shared understanding or definition of community development creates a sense of alignment and mutual support. While community-based initiatives often contribute towards the policy outcomes of several sectors, this raises issues about who owns and takes responsibility for the successful implementation of the whole strategy. Having a clear and coherent community development strategy creates a foundation for co-ordinating activities across sectors and levels, so that different agencies can play their part fairly and effectively.

Too often community development has suffered from the lack of the business case needed to persuade senior officers, funders and politicians that it offers a cost-effective way of delivering higher level results. As we have witnessed over the past few years, it is especially vulnerable to cuts as well as remaining peripheral within government thinking and mainstream public sector organisations.

Orientation

Previous chapters have illustrated how over the years community development has been crucial in spanning the boundary between communities and the state, as well as working across other sectoral or community divisions. As a consequence, some critics have argued that community development has allowed itself to become co-opted into the government's agenda (Pitchford and Henderson, 2008; Craig, 2011). In the past, community development was commonly state-sponsored: workers were either employed directly by local authorities, or their money came via government grants. In the years since we wrote the first edition, government and other major funders, such as the Big Lottery Fund, have tended to use trusted national organisations to manage their major grant programmes at arm's-length, transferring responsibility to external agents, who sometimes operate as consortia to bring together the necessary systems and expertise. This has reignited the recurrent 'in and against the state' debate (LEWRG, 1979), with charges of co-option levelled at some of these agents.

This echoes a perennial dilemma for community development workers. Their role is to support communities in tackling local issues and to do this in ways that are respectful of people's needs and aspirations. And yet most posts are funded by organisations that have their own agendas and priorities such that these workers are answerable to their employers and their objectives need to be achieved. This creates particular difficulties if the projects that the community favours are not in accordance with agency objectives or seem likely to mature too slowly for the timescales imposed by a regime of performance targets. Experienced workers will understand this tension, explain it to all parties and negotiate a way forward that is in accordance with community wishes but also satisfies their employers. Less experienced workers often find it hard to manage this tension and may capitulate to their manager's demands (or else resign).

Community development is fundamentally concerned with power relations, in society at large and at the micro level. It is inevitable, therefore, that workers may find themselves caught in conflicts between those who hold power and those who want or deserve more influence over the conditions of their lives. Dealing with tensions and trouble is inherent to effective practice, and yet not all practitioners have the experience or skills to do this, preferring to suppress conflict rather than devising strategies for resolving it equitably. Developing the personal and collective capacities for mediating conflicts is a neglected aspect of modern community development.

Status and recognition

As this Short Guide has already mentioned, there has been a long-running debate in community development over whether it should be seen as a profession (with all the attendant restrictions regarding entry qualifications and standards) or whether it is more like a social movement, drawing on a network of activists, some of whom are lucky enough to be paid for their work with communities. The latter position reflects community development's rejection of notions of expertise or elitism, and a well-intentioned desire to acknowledge people of all backgrounds for their community development work. Those who take the stance that community development should claim the status of a profession argue that it is an occupation requiring specialist knowledge, sophisticated judgements and dedicated effort, at a level at least equivalent to the work of other recognised professions such as a social work, planning or teaching. Unless community development is understood as a skilled and strategic intervention, it will be seen as amateurish and dispensable.

But without proper training and support, it is in danger of being poorly practised and losing its value base. It is unfortunate that opportunities for learning and qualifications in community development are reducing, with fewer higher education courses running than when we produced the list in the first edition in 2011. Many national organisations are scaling back on training programmes, though the Community Organisers Programme was explicitly designed to support learning through residential and college courses, workshops and web-based blogs for trainees to share their ideas and experiences. In Wales the government has commissioned Community Development Cymru to design and deliver a workforce development strategy to support people working with communities, and this has incorporated community development values into its qualifications framework. The Scottish Community Development Centre (SCDC) provides a range of learning resources and tailored training is offered by some of the other national bodies listed in the Appendix.

There is, however, always a risk that being 'too' professional can be intimidating or off-putting for community members. Community development workers can be seen as representing authority or being the 'experts' and this may generate deference or resentment, which can get in the way of working with communities in ways that value their skills and opinions.

As a result of this unresolved ambivalence, community development continues to be poorly resourced, receiving sporadic support from policy makers and politicians and often relying on the enthusiasm of individual officers or civil servants to ensure that it is even mentioned in reports or policy statements. There is urgent need for community development to be much more firmly embedded across a whole range of policy areas relating to health, wellbeing, social inclusion, civil renewal and community enterprise.

Role boundaries

Paid community developers often find it difficult to explain their function, choosing to blur their role in relation to community members in case it sounds patronising or overly directive. They are generally employed to enable communities to take collective action, to find their voice and to make links with others. This is different from being an activist, representative or leader of the community, but this distinction is not always clearly drawn and indeed sometimes denied, especially where workers identify strongly with the community with whom they are working, perhaps because they live in the area or share key characteristics and interests. Many community development workers are drawn to the role through being active in their own communities, determined to improve life for their families, neighbours and the community to which they feel they belong. This may become a more generalised aspiration to promote greater equality and empowerment, for example, for working class people (Hoggett et al, 2009). They may be driven by compassion or solidarity, possibly framed by human rights or faith perspectives, and this subjective motivation for the work will affect both priorities and direction of progress. It can provide a form of personal conviction that Hoggett and colleagues term 'self-authorisation', enabling people to be both partisan and professional in resolving practice dilemmas that arise from the conflicting interests and social identities that characterise community life.

This is not to say that community development workers must be distant or objective, merely that they should be aware of the boundaries around their role and not inadvertently pursue their own objectives. In her book on networking, Gilchrist refers to the 'seven Es of community development':

- enabling
- encouraging
- empowering
- educating
- equalising

▪ evaluating and
▪ engaging communities to do things for themselves (2009, pp 37–8).

These were devised to highlight the ways in which workers are helping *others* to grow, organise and learn, rather than promoting their own interests or needs. This is important because some community development workers see themselves as indispensable, taking on too many tasks and leaving community members overly dependent on their skills, time and services.

Community belonging: place and identity?

Nowadays people often regard themselves as belonging to more than one community, or even none. Social identities are becoming complicated, reflecting different facets of people's lives, and connections are maintained via social technologies as well as interpersonal relationships. Communities have traditionally been regarded as consisting of 'local' people living or working in a particular locality. In the past, community development was generally organised around area teams or by associating a worker with a 'patch', often of indeterminate size and boundaries. It was presumed that residents would organise or speak up as a local community to improve the quality of life in 'their' area. This was probably a reasonable assumption in the days when people lived, worked, played, socialised, worshipped and learnt together within a few square miles, with plenty of regular interaction between neighbours and workmates. But areas differ enormously in how much they resemble the 'close-knit' communities of imagined yesteryear. The neighbourhoods where community development resources are usually deployed are often places where many residents have not actively chosen to live and yet they usually manage to sustain strong allegiances and a necessary sense of community spirit. Other areas function as little more than way stations or commuter dormitories where there is little sense of place as a unifying bond, with residents rarely meeting and often not even knowing the names of their next-door neighbours.

Where communities do organise locally, this may be as part of an externally imposed government initiative targeted at their 'zone'. There are also frequent examples of NIMBY-ism (not in my backyard), where communities unite against perceived threats such as waste incinerators or plans for a new housing estate. Similarly, attempts to provide sites, hostels or sheltered accommodation (for example, for Travellers, people with learning difficulties, those on bail or people recovering from addiction) are known to generate hostility and fear. This kind of low-level neighbourhood-ism poses dilemmas for the community worker, who, on the one hand, is supposed to support communities on issues that they identify, but who, on the other hand, is also guided by values around treating marginalised people with respect and compassion. In these situations, the community development worker will need to use all their skills in networking, talking and listening to people face-to-face, and building vital levels of trust among all concerned while paying particular attention to issues around power inequalities and social stigma.

Many of the problems experienced by communities are symptomatic of wider structural issues arising from the (global) economy, patterns of migration and government policies. They cannot be solved at local level through projects or relatively short-term interventions. As we saw in Chapter Three, this was the critique first expressed by the Community Development Projects set up in target neighbourhoods in the 1970s. The focus on localism, community action and neighbourhood services apparent in today's government policy, especially in England, presents community development with both opportunities and challenges. In particular, given the impact of austerity cuts on welfare, services and jobs, it will be vital for communities to connect above the local level, so as to understand and tackle the root causes of their problems. These may well be located far away and determined by a distant set of political and economic factors.

Not everyone chooses to engage with local community interests. For some, their most pressing issues may reflect an aspect of their identity that they want to keep private owing to continuing social prejudice or simply because it is not shared by their immediate neighbours. So, for example, a refugee family from Sierra Leone might reasonably prefer to construct their community around fellow West Africans living in this country, and be absorbed in campaigns for better HIV services. Others may associate more frequently with people who share a hobby, such as choral singing, lace-making or football, spending their leisure time away from home and not taking much interest in their place of residence.

People who experience particular forms of discrimination are also more likely to make connections with others in similar predicaments – either because they feel safer in their company or to organise to change things (or both). Black and minority ethnic people have been effective in establishing community and voluntary organisations, alongside faith bodies, and these provide important rallying points for the different communities and form vital alliances against racism.

There is good evidence that members of minority communities who have a strong sense of identity and feel secure in their 'home' cultures are more likely to integrate with the wider population. This 'radical pluralism of identity politics' (Hoggett et al, 2009, p 20) allows people to organise separately in ways that suit their circumstances and address shared community issues before they can confidently join with others in broader movements or mainstream forums. There is a persuasive argument for supporting the setting up of mono-cultural or identity-based organisations that can run activities and specialist services that are appropriate for different ethnicities and faiths (Gilchrist, 2004). However, this strategy can cause resentment and has been challenged by some politicians and policy makers, who assert that it encourages divisions between communities and undermines the cohesion of society. For community development, the challenge is to acknowledge the intersectionality of people's identities (the interaction of different aspects of their lives) and find ways of supporting people to organise around their preferred issues and interests (Gilchrist et al, 2010).

Equality and diversity

On the face of it, the meaning of the term equality may seem fairly obvious and most people understand it as a key component of social justice. However, on closer inspection things become more complicated and there are a number of competing interpretations, which will be outlined here.

Equality is usually linked to ideas of fairness, inclusion and diversity; however, none of these terms have any legal basis, so it is important to be clear about how community development can use these concepts to tackle unfair discrimination and respect differences in order that people can achieve their full potential and participate equally in activities and campaigns. Some approaches favour using a human rights model that refers to a shared commitment to ensuring that all citizens enjoy the same entitlements, for example, to services or opportunities (BRAP, 2015).

Crucially, this does not mean treating everyone the same, and some critics distinguish between equal treatment, equal opportunities and equal outcomes. Equal opportunity recruitment practices strive to ensure that all candidates go through the same selection process by using transparent criteria to review applications and standard questions at interviews. But this model doesn't acknowledge how discrimination and privilege are embedded in society, resulting in deep-rooted disadvantage and social exclusion. Proactive strategies may be required to overcome the barriers and biases that deter or prevent some people from achieving equality of outcomes or exercising free choices. So, for example, community development is justified in using positive action measures to support the self-organisation of minorities (for example, Ryder et al, 2014), make use of positive images and role models to overcome stereotypes and internalised oppression, reach out to marginalised communities, and encourage participation by removing practical barriers.

Another proactive approach, but a more controversial one, is to set targets for representation and inclusion to make absolutely sure that organisations and activities are truly inclusive and that everyone is guaranteed a fair chance to influence the decisions that matter. Some counter that this is unfair, but it seems it may be necessary, as the phrase 'equality of opportunity' has been around for a long time and, despite more than 40 years of legislation, many groups in the UK experience persistent disadvantage (Hills, 2010). In the UK we have what is known as a pan-equalities framework (Equalities Review Team, 2007) which is now enshrined in the Equality Act 2010. Prior to this, different forms of discrimination were dealt with through separate legislation and some were ignored altogether.

The current integrated approach is based on an analysis of how people come to be disadvantaged by looking at what factors restrict the chances of them fulfilling their 'capabilities' in life according to the different equality strands (Sen, 2009). In many instances, disadvantage is correlated with biological features, such as sex, age, skin colour and so on, which render people vulnerable to discrimination or restrict their choices. Other factors are socially determined, such as those prejudices associated with faith, sexual orientation or class background. Different factors tend to interact in people's lives, such that a white professional woman with grown-up children is less likely to be turned down for a job than a younger Asian woman of childbearing age who may suffer from both sexist and racist assumptions about her employability. The pan-equalities approach has been criticised by some equalities communities who argue that it marginalises the social impact of widespread disadvantage affecting whole populations, focusing instead on the experiences and capabilities of individuals. But for community development, it allows flexibility in promoting equality in opportunities and outcomes at a local level in specific circumstances, as well as tackling more pervasive biases and barriers that discourage participation for some sections of the community.

Campaigning for equalities and honouring diversity therefore need to go hand-in-hand. As we saw in Chapter Two, equality is a core value for community development but it can nonetheless be difficult to work out what is fair in any given situation. Historical factors can result in continued disadvantage: for example, the segregated schools system for children with hearing impairments meant that they did not receive the same quality of education as others. Conversely, failure to understand or respect different cultural requirements, such as offering halal food, can exclude people from accessing services such as eldercare.

Community development is concerned with all such issues and has developed a certain level of expertise in tackling discrimination and prejudice (Gilchrist, 2007). These include making sure that the things that deter people from participating in community activities or prevent them from making use of opportunities or services are identified and tackled. Some people are worried about going out at night to attend evening meetings, so it might be a good idea to have gatherings at different times of day or to arrange transport. If people expect hostility or ridicule, they may prefer to meet separately (for example, as a group of older lesbians) instead of engaging in more mainstream activities. Others may need help with their caring responsibilities, perhaps through the provision of a crèche or money to cover short-term respite.

Implementing such measures with limited funding is difficult and can lead to accusations of favouritism or bias towards 'equality groups'. Community development workers who are proactive in tackling inequalities may therefore find themselves criticised. They need to be careful to justify their work with certain groups and to make sure that they cannot be accused of looking after their own interests, especially if they share the same identity, for example, as a woman. Dealing with cultural insensitivity and prejudicial attitudes can be challenging. Somehow a balance must be struck between being supportive towards community members and explaining why certain language or behaviour is regarded as derogatory or hurtful. It is by no means straightforward to ensure inclusivity, diversity and equality in one's work, while simultaneously seeking to promote community empowerment.

Leadership and representation issues

Building the capacity of communities and enabling people to organise collectively means thinking about how leadership operates, how it can be nurtured and whether it fairly represents community wishes. Paradoxically, community leaders are not always the best people to champion community interests, even though they may be hard-working and articulate. Their role can sometimes put them at odds with other members of the community that they purport to represent. This can be for a variety of reasons. They may have become caught up in partnership arrangements, devoting lots of spare time to committees and left with little energy to keep in touch with what ordinary residents want. Or they may be too partisan, interested only in narrow issues or obtaining resources for their favourite groups.

A difficulty may arise when leaders are unwilling to delegate aspects of their role to others or to hand over the reins altogether as this can result in burnout and stagnation. However, research shows that this is less common than might be expected, with community leadership often transferred willingly to successive generations of volunteers and activists (Ockenden and Hutin, 2008). Nonetheless, community development should encourage people to take on leadership roles and try to ensure a style of leadership that is inclusive, collaborative, egalitarian and democratic. Sometimes perfectly capable people lack confidence or feel intimidated by the responsibility of following in the footsteps of a good leader, but with a bit of support and perhaps some training, maybe shadowing the part for a period, they will grow into the role and in turn pass it on to someone else.

Leadership responsibilities do not have to reside with one 'charismatic' individual. Tasks and influence can be shared among people who may be good at different aspects of leadership. Thus power is distributed more evenly and democratically in the group. Community development therefore needs to create conditions where leaders and representatives can emerge through debate and action, building agreement among members to effectively represent or articulate their views, and working with others to turn ideas into action.

Nevertheless, it is sometimes necessary to challenge community leaders because they dominate discussion and are dismissive of ideas that don't match their own. This may not be easy for community members to do themselves, perhaps because of the leader's status or because of misguided loyalty. Community workers can be more objective and possibly more diplomatic, suggesting alternative ways of looking at a situation or encouraging other potential leaders to put themselves forward or to pursue a different course of action. Their role may be to 'hold the ring' while disputes and discussions play out, ensuring that issues are dealt with fairly and civilly, or they may have to act as mediator to get to the bottom of rivalries and help a group to move on.

Unfortunately, what communities say they want is not always feasible or fair. People can act in selfish, prejudiced and defensive ways that exacerbate division and discrimination, rather than fostering community spirit and equality. Individual activists and community leaders may dominate discussions because they are articulate, loud or able to give the most time. This can drown out the quieter, less confident voices, masking or distorting their opinions and potentially misrepresenting majority views. Although community workers can be guilty of these tendencies too, the challenge for the person working with such communities is twofold: first, to build the capacity to debate difficult issues and manage competing interests; second, to ensure that people with more marginal or uncomfortable views can influence decisions, perhaps by acting as their advocate or finding other routes through which they can be heard. Active citizens can be awkward citizens, sometimes showing an 'ugly' face that can be intimidating or cynical but, nevertheless, locally committed and enterprising. Although they may have preferences, workers cannot pick and choose who they work with in a group and must find ways to enable people to collaborate constructively with one another and with decision makers.

Keeping the 'usual suspects' involved while also finding fresh voices who supply alternative perspectives and challenges is a serious, but manageable, challenge. It is helpful to foster continuity but also to encourage new people to develop expertise in certain areas. It is vital that community leaders are able to genuinely represent a full range of community views. This is why accountability is so important for communities and practitioners alike.

Accountability

Community development is often shaped by a complex array of formal and informal accountabilities and workers can easily be pulled in different directions. Employers may expect them to adhere to organisational policies and priorities. Managers, usually closer to the specific project objectives, will want to see progress towards these. Funders, for example, charitable foundations, will usually have their own aims, for which they in turn are answerable to donors. Community members tend to want the worker to respond to their immediate needs and help them to achieve medium term goals: organising events, running a group, sorting out troublesome committees, raising money and so on. Meanwhile, practice is supposed to conform to those values and principles established over the years by peers and professionals, notably around participation, empowerment, learning and equality. In other words, community workers are to assist and enable communities, not simply do things for them. Issues of accountability are further compounded for workers employed by elected authorities such as district or county councils. The tensions between representative and participative democracy are inherent in an electoral system that sees councillors as community leaders and yet desires active engagement of communities in public decision-making processes and service delivery. Community development and community engagement officers have been drawn ever more deeply into the localism and empowerment agendas, helping authorities to set up participatory structures, such as neighbourhood panels or health and wellbeing boards, and are forced to be more strategic in their work with communities due to funding cuts. Consequently, many workers report that they have become embroiled in council bureaucracy and are losing their involvement with grassroots activism.

As earlier chapters have demonstrated, it has never been that clear who 'owns' community development and this confusion continues to the present day. In its early years, community development was often located in education departments (alongside youth work), then as part of 'patch' social work teams, then within health services and regeneration programmes (fostering local economic development and social enterprise). More recently, during the New Labour years, community development has been located in community engagement units, based in a central department and accountable to the chief executive. Changes in government policy and public service spending cuts have rendered these latter posts especially vulnerable and community development teams have been drastically reduced by many local authorities.

This is one of the many challenges facing community development, as the work is often quite isolating and support from colleagues in similar positions can be invaluable. Team working offers opportunities to learn from each other, to receive informal feedback and supervision about practice issues, and tends to be more rewarding, so long as it is well managed and there is sufficient time for discussion. However, as in any field, teams can also be fractious, with workloads unfairly distributed or the discussions dominated by particular individuals. Most community development workers – with their group work skills, shared values and sense of justice – tend to be pretty good at team working. Moreover, because of their boundary-spanning roles, they can make valuable contributions to interdisciplinary, or multi-agency working groups where people from different professions and organisations come together.

Mainstreaming, targeted or specialist work?

It could be argued that the profile of community development has been strengthened by the extent to which it has been recognised as a way of working that increases empowerment and improves engagement. However, the mainstreaming of community development has not allowed it to prove its worth as an effective way of tackling deep-rooted problems. Toolkits such as those provided by SCDC can be extremely useful but there is now a bewildering array of guides and frameworks setting out techniques and competences. There is a consequent danger that core skills and values may become diluted because they allow managers and practitioners to assume that anyone who works with communities or even just works in a community setting is doing community development.

The repertoire of skills, values and roles that characterise good community development comes into its own in deprived neighbourhoods or when working with particularly disadvantaged groups. Yet it is an approach that would benefit all communities, helping them to avoid or deal with many of the issues that occur when volunteers or small community groups come together to organise collectively to plan for future improvements, deliver services or influence wider decisions. Community development still needs to present convincing evidence that it offers a unique and valuable service, particularly in relation to reaching target groups who are 'underserved' and 'seldom heard' by mainstream providers.

Demonstrating impact: measuring the social return

There is a great deal of interest in showing that investment in communities yields results (social returns) and yet it has long proved difficult to attribute changes (specific outputs as well as intangible outcomes) to specific inputs or interventions, especially for community development. This is partly about timescales and the importance of moving at a pace dictated by community circumstances and capacity – which means that projects may take years to agree and realise significant goals. But difficulties in demonstrating and claiming impact are also related to the complex conditions in which much community development takes place. Residents move in and out of areas, their lives often in constant flux, while individual and community-level outcomes are affected by a wide range of sometimes contradictory policies and programmes that undermine what community development is trying to achieve.

By its nature, community development tends to operate behind the scenes and often in conjunction with a number of other partners, not least community members themselves. It is inherently difficult to predict what is going to happen and how or when the benefits will appear because there are many people involved, often on a voluntary basis, who are accountable to numerous bodies or sometimes to no one at all. Furthermore, progress depends on a range of factors, most of which are not controlled by either the community or the community development workers. For example, a successful event might be dependent on obtaining funding, good weather, a favourable vote on the council or a sufficient number of volunteers turning up. At the macro level, community economic development projects to promote enterprise and 'job readiness' may be completely derailed by the loss of a major employer. Similarly, sudden demographic changes, such as the arrival of new refugee or migrant worker communities, can undermine (or at least delay) strategies for good community relations, at least until the newcomers are properly settled and integrated.

Community development claims to improve the quality of life for people, especially disadvantaged groups, by helping them to engage with services, increase their influence over decision making and generally lead healthier, happier lives. Statutory employers of community development workers usually expect evidence that plans have been delivered and that things have improved in line with their policy goals or nationally imposed targets, for example, in relation to educational attainment or employment. New managerialism, an approach that came to prominence in the 1990s and which we refer to elsewhere in this Guide, adopted a model of linear progress that could be measured through pre-planned outputs and the achievement of specified targets. Some managers of community development strategies imagined that the performance of their teams could be monitored in this way but failed to take into account the complexity of the work. Nor did they understand that community development is primarily concerned with the issues that communities decide are important and implementing the strategies that they identify as meeting their needs (Miller, 2008). Some funders, especially those using a logic framework model, require applicants to state their expected outputs and milestones and demand regular updates showing progress towards these, even though the actual outcomes are necessarily uncertain or still vague.

In these circumstances it is simply not feasible to plan and predict detailed objectives. In fact, too much focus on predetermined targets would reduce the responsiveness inherent in good community development. Communities change their collective minds about what they want to achieve and which issues they want to prioritise. Their aspirations evolve over time as they learn from their own successes and the experiences of others. The funding and policy context also shapes the feasibility of different options, so community workers need to be alert and flexible in their approach.

Nevertheless, if community development is to be taken seriously as a strategic and professional intervention, then it must be able to show what difference it makes for communities and how this delivers desired policy and social outcomes. There are several recognised models for evaluating the work, with perhaps the most common being the ABCD (Achieving Better Community Development) framework (Barr and Hashagen, 2000). This was originally devised by SCDC and has been extensively used and refined, most recently to become the Learning, Evaluation and Planning toolkit LEAP (www.scdc.org.uk/what/LEAP). It takes as its starting point an ideal vision of a strong and empowered community that is liveable, sustainable and equitable. This translates into five 'quality of life' dimensions around shared wealth, caring, safety, creativity and citizenship. These, in turn, are supported by four building blocks of personal empowerment, positive action, community organisation and participation. The challenge for management, practitioners and communities themselves is to identify the performance criteria that can be used to evaluate the contribution that community development makes towards implementing these outcomes.

One guiding principle is to focus on improvements at community level, rather than individual rewards. Do people generally have less fear of crime? Does the refurbished village hall act as a community anchor building? Are relations between young people and the older generation more cordial and respectful? Have incidents of racial harassment declined? There should be shared gains, although individuals directly involved will almost certainly benefit more because of their enhanced skills, confidence, networks and opportunities.

There are many examples of toolkits designed to assess progress, but until recently there have been very few that are based on communities defining goals for themselves. This is beginning to change, with more willingness to involve communities in using participatory and co-design research techniques to make an initial appraisal of community needs and assets, formulate their own theory of change and then assess how things have developed. For example, as we saw in Chapter Six, rather than depending on formal statistics, Big Local communities are encouraged to use a variety of media (photos, film, song, etc.) to tell the story of their 'journey', including its successes and failures. This qualitative approach may not seem as rigorous as using definite figures but in community development terms it is rooted in residents' visions for change and is ultimately more inclusive and empowering.

Professional standards and ethics

In Chapter Two we emphasised that community development can best be seen as a set of principles that govern the processes of working towards social change and collective capacity building. A major challenge for community development continues to revolve around the balance between how the work is done (that is, in accordance with community development values) and the accomplishment of specific goals. Sometimes there can be a tension between what individuals want and what might seem best for the wider community. Just as in the case of flawed leadership, community development workers are regularly faced with conflicting, often unacknowledged and unresolved, interests and different ideas about how to proceed. Contrary to popular thinking, community is rarely about 'unity', and the principles of community development are not always able to give a clear indication of the best course of action. As indicated in Chapter Five, practitioners need to think on their feet, using their discretion to make ethical and political judgements about what they should (or shouldn't) do.

The latest National Occupational Standards talk about the 'skills, values and processes required for effective and appropriate practice' (FCDL, 2015). Although they are not designed exclusively for professional community development workers, they provide a useful reference point for assessing whether a practitioner is acting within the roles of community development work. There are many routes into professional (paid) community development work and an array of qualifications. While this can be an advantage, opening doors for activists and volunteers, there needs to be coherent training provision and perhaps a body to regulate and validate qualifications at each level. However, it would run counter to a deeply embedded ethos for community development to become overly professionalised or for occupational standards to act as a kind of straitjacket, restricting how people can perform the role and possibly stifling learning and innovation. There is a critical difference between the expectations set out as a form of professionalism, and the kinds of formal qualifications and ethics that accompany professionalisation and control entry into a closed occupational elite.

Brief conclusion

As this Short Guide has shown, community development enjoys various perspectives and applications. It has been harnessed for many purposes, not all of which sit comfortably with its espoused principles. Its emphasis on high-level, but often intangible outcomes, such as community spirit or cohesion, has lent it a certain ambiguity about what it achieves on a day-to-day basis or through specific projects. Community development claims to tackle the causes of major social problems, but often makes little headway. It can appear mired in dealing with the symptoms of poverty and conflict endemic in our unequal society. Only by maintaining a critical and reflexive praxis that links theory, politics and practice, will those engaged in community development work ensure that their efforts and skills make a difference to social justice in the long term (Shaw, 2004; Ledwith and Springett, 2010; Ledwith, 2011).

Community development is probably best regarded as an approach to social change that is carried out under many auspices by people in several different roles: the paid specialist community development worker, other community-oriented professionals, social entrepreneurs, volunteers, community members, politically motivated activists, charity workers, elected councillors and a whole range of people who simply want to make life better for individuals and communities, such as artists, faith leaders and school governors.

The ambiguities, dilemmas and challenges set out in this chapter reflect but also blur the core values and competences that define community development. As we will examine in the final chapter, its future is not clear; yet it draws on a tradition of practice and theory, in the UK and across the world, that will ensure its continuing relevance to social progress and democracy.

Summary

- The status and purpose of community development is often obscured by political rhetoric and role ambiguity.
- It is poorly recognised because it embodies processes that take time to mature and its impact is difficult to demonstrate among other changes at community level.
- Community development works with communities of interest as well as place. These are often not tied to specific localities and may enable communities who feel marginalised or who share a particular political or cultural identity to organise together.
- Work to promote equality and diversity is an important aspect of community development and poses a number of challenges.
- Community development supports a model of shared leadership and is concerned with complex issues of representation and accountability.

■ Its value base provides a significant foundation for setting standards and guiding practice.

Further reading

The dilemmas of development work (Hoggett et al, 2009) examines how practitioners operate in uncertain situations where their personal experience and values provide the necessary 'compass'. Pitchford and Henderson's (2008) book poses important challenges for community development as a profession while making some key recommendations for future debate.

As mentioned in earlier chapters, national organisations such as the Federation for Community Development Learning and the Scottish Community Development Centre are routes into interesting current debates and reflections on the state of community development in the UK. It is worth visiting the websites of the organisations mentioned in the Appendix to find out about latest opportunities and challenges.

8

future prospects

This chapter considers likely trends in the external environment over the immediate future, what community development can offer in response to these trends and how they, in turn, are likely to affect community development. It ends by asking what they mean for the evolution of community development as an occupation and approach in the coming years.

Developments since 2011

The first edition of this Short Guide was written shortly after the UK Coalition government had come to power. After a decade or more of strategic partnerships, which brought communities into a range of new governance arrangements and put significant funds into disadvantaged communities, the incoming government's Big Society pledged to give communities more powers and transfer control downwards from the political centre to local decision-making bodies.

The judgement of some, at least in the community policy field, was that community development under the New Labour regime had become co-opted and professionalised – top down rather than bottom up. For them, this change of direction offered an opportunity to give residents themselves the lead in addressing local issues. However, Coalition policies to transfer more services from the state to communities, coupled with austerity measures, which hit the poorest hardest, gave cause for considerable concern. Neoliberal commitments to the market, to enterprise and to individual and community responsibility had persisted under New Labour, but now they were no longer encumbered by social democratic principles. The Coalition government continued to support a range of community initiatives to encourage social action, albeit with considerably less funding, and the one-party Conservative government that took power in 2015 retains a commitment to a 'Bigger and Stronger Society' (Cabinet Office, 2015). Nevertheless, the predominant discourse has been of community rights, social enterprise, volunteering and the transfer of services. This is the case even in the devolved administrations, consistently to the political left of the UK government, though equally affected by its austerity economics. So while community is still on the agenda, it is a much more self-reliant community that policies seek to promote today.

Meanwhile, the other historical trends we observed remain salient. The evidence for climate change is still disputed but, as we say in Chapter Six, attitudes, habits and practices are changing – albeit slowly. The threat of terrorism looms large, while the mass exodus by refugees fleeing violence, civil war and persecution in parts of Africa and the Middle East is posing new challenges to surrounding countries and to Europe.

Communications technology continues to advance at lightning speed. And while the recession of 2008/09 seems to have run its course, the global economy remains far from stable at the time of writing, with the financial markets nervous over the fate of the Chinese economy and much debate over the European Union's handling of successive national debt crises.

We do not intend in this final chapter to try to predict the future. Just a glance at the fate of past predictions suggests that this is a dangerous game. Nevertheless, as this short review suggests, we can identify current trends in the external environment that present both dangers and opportunities for community development in 2016. Many of these have already been flagged up in earlier chapters. Some mirror or build on those we identified in 2011 – others are new:

- neoliberal globalisation and austerity
- the shrinking public sphere
- migration and the changing significance of place
- the digital age
- changing politics
- climate change.

Neoliberal globalisation

Rather than acting as a wake-up call on global economic models, the financial crisis of 2008/09 appears to have reinforced neoliberal approaches to the economy across most of the globe. Neoliberalism brings with it the dominance of the market and the shrinking of the state as well as massive deregulation of trade and labour relations. For community development, the danger today is that it becomes complicit in the dominance of the market, shepherding communities into becoming entrepreneurs and taking services over from the state, either on contract from the state or as volunteers.

Meanwhile, the neoliberal prescription for economic recovery post-recession has been one of austerity policies, which continue to have a disproportionate impact on the disadvantaged communities that are the focus of so much community development work (Beatty and Fothergill, 2013). The gap between rich and poor continues to widen. The UK is fourth on the scale of income inequality in OECD countries and it is the only G7 country where the gap has widened since the beginning of the century, with the richest 10% owning over half the nation's wealth (Credit-Suisse, 2014). As Chapter Three remarked, the restructuring of the labour market through low wages and zero-hours contracts means that the policy discourse of strivers and hard-working families versus skivers simply does not hold water, with many hard-working families on benefits and living in poverty. And yet, there is little to suggest that this gloomy picture will change. As Marris and Rein commented nearly five decades ago (1967), there seem to be few votes in initiatives or policies to help the most disadvantaged in society.

Poorer communities are often dependent on the state for both for employment opportunities and for services that are themselves facing heavy cuts. Current economic pressures will only reinforce trends that have concentrated the most vulnerable people in society in the poorest housing, creating a spiral of local disadvantage in terms of unemployment, poor health, low educational attainment, access to legal services and so on. Cuts in housing benefits are displacing many poorer families from the communities where they now live, sending them many miles away from their support networks and disrupting their children's education.

Housing policy – or the lack of it – means that housing and shelter is now seen as an investment market rather than a public service or human right. There have been a number of high profile cases over recent months where families have been evicted from prime sites in order to make way for prestigious developments. And concern is mounting over the growing number of properties that have been bought by overseas investors only to lie empty. Right to Buy for council tenants is now to be extended to housing associations, despite the fact that many of those homes bought since the policy was introduced have become buy-to-let properties. For many people, the English aspiration to buy their own home has become a pipedream. The alternative to a reduced stock of social housing is insecure and only loosely regulated private rental accommodation. The short-term tenancies that result are no recipe for 'community', while high turnover and the fear of eviction means that private tenants are very difficult to organise.

There is a strong rhetoric of localism in current policy that talks of bringing services closer to the people who use them. However, the market, as we have seen, favours economies of scale. Where local services are not being closed as a result of public spending cuts, they are being withdrawn instead by businesses seeking to rationalise their operations, as is the case with rural bus routes. Ever more rigid procurement systems pose challenges even to the larger, more established community organisations. For small organisations without reserves, the prospect of entering this market is almost non-existent.

In recent decades, the virtues of voluntary and community organisations as alternative providers to the state have been extolled with substantial funding for capacity building and contract delivery. But now cuts in public spending threaten this investment. The infrastructure on which many smaller community groups depend has been particularly hard hit, especially at national level. A recent report on the third sector's financial viability found that its income had flat-lined since 2009, despite the economic recovery, with small and medium sized charities hardest hit, and with income from individuals 'unlikely to compensate for the falls in income from government sources' (NCVO, 2015).

Even where it is not being cut, the likelihood is that community development funding from any public or other institutional source will be expected to produce efficiency savings and that funding will increasingly be dependent on proving 'impact' – a slippery term at the best of times and one that is difficult to apply to the kinds of 'soft', intangible outcomes that community development produces or, indeed, the timescales it requires. Work to explore ways of capturing social returns on investment has been going on for some time; it has yet to deliver on its promise, although there may be considerable potential here to build the business case for community development (NEF, 2010). More needs to be done, however, to show how accounting for social value can be made to work in practice and to test and consolidate innovative ideas in this field. In the meantime, it will be important to ensure that competition for scarce funding does not inhibit co-operation in the search for more creative solutions.

This is a bleak picture. However, it is important to remember that three quarters of voluntary and community organisations have no relationship with a government funder. This includes the many smaller, informal groups to be found 'under the radar', especially those in rural areas and those organised by black and minority communities (McCabe et al, 2010). Where they do have or aspire to have such a relationship, new EU rules, along with the government's Public Services (Social Value) Act 2012, have the potential to create a more level playing field – if taken seriously. But this will depend on training for the officials applying the rules and making choices, as well as a relaxation of some of the more formal requirements. Meanwhile, for those who believe that community development has become too dependent on public sector funding, there are new opportunities. A range of new programmes and agencies now seek to build social investment in the UK, while private trusts and foundations are exploring new forms of financial support. There is also potential for innovative ideas in crowdfunding and similar internet mechanisms. Meanwhile, organisations like Citizens UK and the newly formed ACORN branches in England are demonstrating what can be done without state funding, through the resources of faith communities, schools, trade unions and other organisations.

The current interest in social enterprise offers another way forward, as we saw in Chapter Six. Again, there are well-documented pitfalls, especially where the need to raise money on the private market trumps the social bottom line. The experience of the social housing sector in the UK demonstrates the challenges in this respect. Here, the need to attract market finance has led to increasing economies of scale. Mergers and consolidation have led to increasing centralisation among UK voluntary housing associations, which, like community development corporations in the US, have also been criticised for behaving more and more like private enterprises (Purkis, 2012).

This is not inevitable. While there are challenges, there are also positive lessons to take from the considerable experience of enterprise and asset ownership to date. The Scottish community-based housing association movement retains its roots, and there are also many examples of ordinary people using their initiative, local resources and knowledge of community markets to set up co-operatives and community enterprises that are innovative and income generating, while also meeting locally defined social needs. Growing a business that can generate income for reinvestment requires determination and support – social investment is still a drop in the ocean. Nonetheless, increased interest in sustainable development and social innovation, along with the search for new economic models, may offer promising signs for the future.

Community development can contribute a great deal to this agenda. It can support groups in assessing whether to take up opportunities to engage in enterprise and take on assets, so that they can make informed decisions. It can also pass on the lessons from past experience. If communities are to gain the maximum advantage from these opportunities, community development workers will also need to engage with leading thinking on this front and with innovative entrepreneurs, exploring ways of working creatively with private business and new financial arrangements. But community development will also have an important role to play in monitoring the impact of new developments on all parts of the community and ensuring that groups who pursue this agenda remain firmly rooted in, and accountable to, their foundations in the community.

The shrinking state: preserving the public sphere

The state is the fall guy in much political rhetoric today. In a decade when many governments are committed to reducing the role of the state, can communities take on all the responsibilities demanded of them, especially communities already under pressure? A world where civil society reigns unchecked is unlikely to be the romantic utopia its advocates imagine. The mediating hand of the state is needed to balance competing interests, support the unorganised, ensure accountability and so on. The rolling back of the state also presents a challenge to many community development workers – at least in advanced democracies – who see it as the ultimate guarantor of equalities and social justice. However, there are new statutory opportunities emerging in Scotland and Wales around civic engagement, governance and citizen empowerment, and it will be important that communities are sufficiently organised to take advantage of these.

The promise of more powers to communities is, in essence, one we should welcome. Certainly, this is a prospect that will be attractive to many at local level. However, it does come with a number of health warnings. One is that resources are not evenly distributed. A number of studies over the years have shown volunteering to be higher in affluent than in low-income neighbourhoods, who may therefore be doubly disadvantaged by calls for more voluntary action. There are dangers that communities will be set up to fail, expected to take on services and assets that others have not managed to provide successfully. Adequate resources and guidance will be at a premium.

The fragmentation of service delivery in the hands of a growing variety of providers and procurers will also raise major questions about accountability. The contracting out of services already means that it is more and more difficult to know who to hold responsible when things go wrong. Paradoxically, however, contract specifications may lead to more rather than less centralised control. Over the years, increased regulation has also hit communities hard as they struggle to implement health and safety regulations, criminal checks and burdensome monitoring schemes, as well as to escape an increasingly litigious society, with the media waiting to pounce on any infringement.

There may have been good initial reasons behind all of these measures (for example, to manage risk or ensure proper financial accountability) and successive governments have made commitments to cut red tape. However, the unintended consequences of these regulations and associated assumptions have been considerable. Most men, for example, will need to think very hard nowadays before volunteering to work with children. Volunteers may be put off by the need to obtain the necessary certificates for food hygiene standards before being allowed to run a jam and cake stall to raise money for a local good cause. Insofar as litigation has replaced traditional forms of accountability, it has created an increasingly risk-averse society and is, in any case, not a realistic option for the poorest and most disenfranchised in society. Legal aid has been severely cut and class actions, for example, are difficult to pursue under UK law.

If this seems unduly negative, the examples in previous chapters tell the story of how much can be achieved by community development, often in partnership with, or with the support of the state. Moves towards co-production – at individual and community level – offer new opportunities that allow communities to contribute to the production of local goods and services as they see fit (Durose and Richardson, 2015). There are very positive examples of community-run services to learn from and there are also important lessons from the past about what works and what doesn't. Distilling and applying these lessons is something that community workers are well placed to do, helping to ensure that community-run services are appropriate, responsive, inclusive and accountable. Supporting communities to make their voices heard when services are threatened or do not meet their needs will also continue to be a priority, through finding creative ways of holding external services and other actors to account, especially for those in communities whose needs are not adequately or appropriately met.

Some argue that it is not only the state that is shrinking but the whole of the public sphere. Physical public spaces where people could mix with people unlike themselves are now often privatised or felt to be unsafe. Community centres, open access leisure and sports facilities, adult education, public parks and libraries are suffering from the cuts or are themselves being privatised. We also commented earlier on the disappearance of the traditional spaces where citizens could discuss public issues and learn political skills at local level. We cannot return to the past – and, in any case, some of these institutions had their own failings. But community development needs to take on the challenge of creating new gathering places, new spaces for dialogue and debate in and across the most disadvantaged communities.

Some current programmes offer these opportunities. The government was surprisingly hands-off when it funded the Community Organisers Programme in England and, though much of its work was small scale, it has given birth to a range of interesting initiatives. Examples cited in this Short Guide include the innovative introduction of an Organisation Workshop programme based on a model developed in the global South (Box 6.8) and the formation of an ACORN branch which has lobbied successfully for an ethical lettings policy at local authority level (Box 6.1). In addition, the programme has spawned a number of new community interest companies which are disseminating community organising in their various regions. A report on the programme's legacy suggests that it has planted seeds which we have yet to see germinate (Imagine, 2015). The Big Local programmes across the UK represent a significant investment over time in their beneficiary communities and the fruits of new kinds of social investment have yet to be seen. Independent organisations like Citizens UK continue to achieve successes that will improve individual lives, for example, the introduction of the living wage across London.

Redefining community: migration and its significance for place

Wars, climate change, the destruction of habitats, global media, cheaper travel, the opening up of markets – all have, in their different ways, contributed to the movement of people over recent years, reconfiguring national populations and local communities across the planet.

However, while some borders have opened, others have closed. Anti-immigration moral panics illustrate the 'dark side' of community and responding with 'tough' policies on border control has always been an easy mark for politicians seeking popular support. Demographic and cultural change has been a permanent feature of some urban communities, but it is likely to affect a wider range of areas in the future (Taylor and Wilson, 2015). Meanwhile, these changes have fuelled a rise in far-right organising and nationalist political parties in many European countries.

Community development has an important role to play in promoting co-operation and mutual understanding. But the need to foster solidarity and build bridges between suspicious communities will continue to provide a challenge, especially as austerity bites further, as people seek someone to blame, and as parts of the media – as well as politicians – fan divisions. Divide and rule has always been a powerful tool and uncertainty breeds defensiveness. Responding effectively to change will need creativity in bringing people together around common issues: creating space for informal encounters and conversations, and using the enormous potential of social media and the internet. It will involve working with both new and 'host' communities to build the confidence that they need to reach across social divisions and find ways of recognising and addressing the fears on which suspicion is built (see Chapter Seven).

Box 8.1 Finding common ground

A community organiser from the Community Organisers Programme spoke of challenging racist behaviour on the doorstep, but also consistently asking probing 'why' questions in order to keep a dialogue going, rather than to condemn. He also described how complaints about the use of local services had initially brought racial tensions to the surface but that now different groups were working together.

Some white residents had been talking about 'the Somalians' misusing communal facilities in their block. When pressed, they described it as the behaviour of 'some' Somalis, and, when it came down to it, they found that some people from the Somali community actually shared their concerns. They were then able to work together to resolve the issue and campaign for better provision from the council. This was a light-bulb moment: witnessing how creating a shared interest could transcend cultural differences. 'They don't mix socially and probably never will. But they work well together and are making progress on the issue concerned.'

Adapted from Taylor and Wilson (2016)

Shifting patterns of migration and settlement present further, quite different challenges for community development. In their discussion of the future for community development in the US, DeFilippis and Saegert (2012) argue that immigration is transforming the meanings of both community and development, as communities become increasingly multi-ethnic and transnational. Thus, they ask: if a Mexican-American community pools money to build a community centre in its members' town of origin in Puebla, does this contribute to community development in their home city of Chicago? Will the notion of community, as a result, become even more detached from place? If so, what will this mean for community development?

To announce the death of the local is premature. Localism is part of current political rhetoric and place is still significant for many people, a view that is backed up by recent surveys. For disadvantaged communities with little bridging social capital, it is particularly important. But place is now one source of identity among many. Research has illustrated the complexity and ingenuity that people use to construct social identities. Identities are used strategically to create a sense of safety, to seek integration and to assert rights, for example, in relation to sexual orientation or disability (Wetherell, 2009). Ethnic origin and citizenship are not straightforwardly aligned, leading to hybrid identities that combine nationality with other characteristics, such as British Muslim. Similarly, cultural patterns of oppression are interrelated and the nature of this intersectionality needs to be understood. Community development must take into account these more complicated patterns of belonging and be aware of the power differentials and political perspectives associated with them (Gilchrist et al, 2010).

The digital age

It is a truism to say that digital technology has revolutionalised the way we live now, changing the way we access information and the way we communicate. It remains to be seen whether younger people, who have grown up with social media and mobile phones, will understand notions of community, place, identity and organisation in the same ways as previous generations. As traditional public spaces disappear, will cyberspaces and online social networks replace them? Will blogs and Twitter – or platforms yet to be invented – replace the letters pages of local newspapers or public meetings in the village hall? The communications revolution has enabled globalisation from below, by giving communities in different parts of the world the means to communicate easily with each other. It has changed the meaning of community, as it allows for instant communication between indigenous communities and friends and family in the diaspora. Political parties now campaign through new technology as well as traditional public meetings and protests. Social media have also enabled the speedy organisation of global protest and disaster relief. As ownership of the more established media becomes more and more concentrated and controlled, spaces like the Twittersphere open communication and influence out to ever more people.

On a more local scale, digital technology has introduced new ways of mobilising people and made it possible to expand and strengthen local activity, with virtual messaging and meetings supplementing face-to-face communication. Communities and citizens can access and share information on a scale unimagined in the early 1990s. Social networking sites allow groups to keep in touch with their members, let them know about their activities and mobilise support for campaigns. New virtual networks are being set up all the time to bring people together, connect communities with each other and notify members about developments locally, nationally and across the globe. An increasing number of local websites operate as digital community newspapers (see, for example, www.streetlife.org), while sites such as Avaaz (www.avaaz.org) and Indymedia (www.indymedia.org.uk) keep people informed of national and international developments.

Box 8.2 Connecting online

One example of an online community is Vibewire, a youth-led not-for-profit born on the streets of Sydney in 2000. It acts as a dynamic connection point between young people and the arts, culture, business and ideas, and describes itself as a launch pad for young change-makers (www.vibewire.org). While it is very much an online organisation, it also organises regular face-to-face events in the Sydney area and has developed a physical hub, which acts as a business incubator for young social entrepreneurs to develop new start-up ventures. While it could be described as a social enterprise,

> it is 'far removed from the business model of entrepreneurship, showing little regard for profit or formal business tools'. It is collaborative rather than competitive and highly democratic in its form of organisation.
>
> Adapted from Kenny et al (2015, pp 196–7)

As we will see in the following section, this has opened the way to new forms of activism and campaigning.

Nothing comes without a price. There are downsides to this fantastic new resource. One is the issue of digital exclusion. Those who are not on top of the latest developments risk being left out and left behind. This is in part a question of access to resources, but new skills are required too: in filtering and retrieving information, keeping safe and protecting privacy, navigating perpetually changing technologies, and designing the message and its medium. Digital spaces are open to censorship and appropriation and surveillance by the powerful. The advantages listed earlier carry their own risks too: information becomes ephemeral and vulnerable to manipulation; identities and loyalties can become attenuated and fragmented, especially if they cease to be anchored offline. There is a 'dark side' to the internet, from trolling to online sexual exploitation.

Community resources and peer-to-peer skills exchanges can help to combat problems of digital exclusion. Community development needs to learn how to exploit the new technologies – especially social networking – to nurture connections and complement face-to-face interaction. Nevertheless, the evidence from research into local digital networks suggests that people use these extremely effectively to post information about community activities, to arrange meetings with other residents and generally to maintain the foundations of community life. Fears that virtual communication will replace the face-to-face, so far, seem unfounded.

A new politics?

With the exception of devolution, attempts in the UK to change the formal political system have been unsuccessful. A referendum on proportional representation yielded a resounding no vote, commitments to reform the House of Lords were shelved and even the referendum on Scottish independence resulted in a return to the status quo. A brief flirtation with a Coalition government ended with an emphatic return to single-party government.

But this is only part of the story, as we saw in Chapter Three. The Scottish referendum in 2014 had an exceptionally high turnout and the unprecedented interest in politics there, especially among young people, took many by surprise. And it has not been a one-off. Although the UK now has a one-party government, there was a surge in votes for the smaller parties in the 2015 general election across the political spectrum – particularly the Scottish National Party (left of centre) and the relatively new UK Independence Party (right of centre). The victory of the Conservative Party also led to a surge in membership for the other two main parties. Nor has the election of a new leader for the defeated Labour Party gone to plan, with a left-wing candidate elected, despite initially being considered a rank outsider, following packed meetings across the country (including Scotland, where the 2015 general election removed most Scottish Labour MPs from their seats). As we said in Chapter Three, while all this suggests disillusionment with the way formal politics is run in the UK, it certainly does not imply apathy.

We have already alluded to the success of Citizens UK in England in putting issues such as the Living Wage on the political agenda and bringing together alliances for change. We have also referred to the growth of ACORN, another radical community organising movement, which, in the 15 months since the first UK branch was established in Bristol in 2014, has acquired 12,000-plus supporters, with new branches setting up at the time of writing.

A new politics is also developing through the internet and social media. Campaigning organisations such as 38 Degrees in the UK, GetUp! in Australia, Avaaz internationally, and others, have mobilised a new form of activism to attract signatories to petitions aimed at raising the profile of a range of issues. While this is dubbed by some as 'clicktivism', these organisations have also taken the opportunities offered by having a large and growing list of supporters, to mobilise people to take action around their campaigns at a local level. Protest groups such as Occupy have been able to communicate through Facebook, Twitter and other social media platforms across the world to set up and co-ordinate local demonstrations and occupations, connecting up across continents. The internet allows communities to 'act local, think global' by finding out what groups in other parts of the world are doing and sharing ideas. These technologies are, of course, particularly potent in mobilising young people, a section of the population that community groups do not always find it easy to engage. Meanwhile, mainstream political parties are increasingly using the internet to mobilise support, following the example of Barack Obama's 2007/08 presidential campaign.

Climate change and sustainable development

Chapter Six described the contribution that community development can make to the sustainable development challenge. As we saw, the phrase 'think globally, act locally' originated in relation to environmental concerns. Forecasts of extreme weather conditions remind us of the tremendous costs that will be – and are being – borne by communities. There seems to be agreement that climate change has led to an increase in hurricanes and typhoons, but even where there is doubt, research suggests that global warming increases their impact (Trenberth et al, 2015). Although nature is no respecter of class, it is still often the poorest communities that suffer most from environmental degradation and disaster, or who end up living near the industrial or waste processing facilities that cause damage to health and wellbeing that can last over generations.

The search for alternative energy sources has brought new resources to communities – in Scotland, for example, wind is a valuable resource and can bring significant funding into an area (see Box 6.5). But the expansion of wind farms has also divided communities and raised questions about how far the money is being used to benefit communities.

We have commented earlier on the notion of community 'resilience'. While the origins of this discourse lie in the field of disaster relief and prevention, the use of the term has since been applied to sustainable development and now to the economic challenges that face people in the poorest communities. This takes us back to where we began: the global economy. Indeed, the equitable distribution and preservation of the planet's resources has been an important driver in the search for alternative economic forms and demonstrates the interrelatedness of the issues discussed here and elsewhere.

The challenge for community development, as we argued in Chapter Six, is to convince communities that they have a role to play – that they can do something themselves. For, while local 'clean and green' issues are often top of their agenda, the challenges of climate change often seem distant and beyond their control. Much larger forces are at work in causing global warming and environmental degradation, but the search for solutions requires actions at every level, from the transnational to the very local.

Bringing it all together

We have reflected at several points in this Short Guide on the ways in which interest in and support for community development have ebbed and flowed over time. Community development has had to reinvent itself to suit political and ideological circumstances, and different models have come to the fore at different times and in different settings. Indeed, this constant reinvention is reflected in debates about what language we should use to describe it. Community development has evolved a chameleon-like nature, which helps it to survive, but this means that it can appear to take on the characteristics of other approaches or merge into the background and disappear altogether.

At its best, however, this adaptability allows community development to take a holistic and flexible approach, placing it in a good position to help communities and those working with them to address the challenges of the future. The complexity of society today requires brokers or intermediaries who can work, as John Gaventa put it, 'on both sides of the [power] equation' (2003). This role, working across community and sectoral boundaries, requires particular strengths in dealing with competing demands and conflicting loyalties, but also in accepting that the 'boundary spanner' will often be perceived as 'not one of us' by both sides, despite his or her best efforts (Howard and Taylor, 2010).

This takes us back to another of the debates we referred to in our Introduction, as to whether community development is an approach, a role, a profession or a movement. Over the decades, there have been fierce debates about values and the risk that these will be eroded if community development is used in an instrumental way or co-opted into government (or indeed any other external) agendas. The sense of community development as a movement, which was prevalent in the 1970s, seemed largely absent when we wrote our first edition, at least in England, although the Community Organisers Programme described itself as training for social action, and creating a movement was clearly one of its aspirations. However, at present, organisations adopting different approaches to community development – from Nurture Development, which supports ABCD, through Citizens UK and NatCAN (National Community Activists Network), to the Community Organisers Programme and its successor body COLtd – may work separately and, in some cases, competitively. There is little sense of the kind of support infrastructure and collaboration achieved in the past by the Community Sector Coalition or the Community Development Exchange. Of the UK countries, Scotland perhaps has the strongest infrastructure but, with devolution, national programmes tend to run separately across the different countries, reducing the scope for cross-border learning. Too often, national programmes also operate in separate silos at local level, although where opportunities for synergies have been taken, this has been beneficial.

There should be no contradiction between seeing community development as a movement with values, while at the same time demanding a professional and skilled approach. There will always be a spectrum of models and standards. Whatever the approach taken, it is important that community development is embedded in a clear ethical framework and adopts a reflexive stance towards the opportunities and dilemmas inherent in the work.

Summary

- Austerity, coupled with a reduction of the role of the state, is likely to hit the poorest communities particularly hard. Climate change is already having the greatest impact on these communities.
- Community development has a role in the application of new and sustainable local economic approaches, in supporting communities to run their own services and public spaces, and in exploring new forms of co-production.
- However, if these are to work for all parts of the community, community development needs to retain its role in supporting community voice, to preserve and renew the resources and services these communities can ill afford to lose, to hold emerging types of provision accountable and to work with allies to tackle the external factors that hold these communities back.
- Community development will also need to build on its networking role, engaging with new providers and decision-makers from all sectors to make services work with and for local people.
- Community development will need to acknowledge and work with new kinds of communities as changing migration patterns and the digital age change the meaning of collective identities and weaken, or perhaps change, the significance of locality.
- As the public sphere shrinks, community development also has an important role in creating new spaces for dialogue and democratic debate.

- New technologies create exciting new opportunities for communication and public debate but, like most magic bullets, they have their pitfalls. Community development cannot afford to be left behind in this revolution or in understanding its implications.
- Community development's adaptability will be at a premium in meeting these new challenges. But it needs to be embedded in a strong ethical framework, critical reflexivity and a good understanding of the skills and values needed to work for social justice in the poorest communities.

Further reading

The think tanks are the best resource for research on new opportunities and trends. The New Economics Foundation (NEF), Demos, Nesta (National Endowment for Science, Technology and the Arts), the RSA (Royal Society of Arts) and Involve (involve.org.uk) are all important thought leaders, looking at futures in citizenship, governance, new economic models and the environment. *The Road Ahead* is an annual analysis by NCVO (the National Council for Voluntary Organisations) of the changing operating environment for the voluntary and community sector.

references

Aiken, M. (2014) *Ordinary glory: Big surprise not big society*, London: National Coalition for Independent Action.

Aiken, M., Cairns, B., Taylor, M. and Moran, R. (2011) *Community organisations controlling assets: A better understanding*, York: Joseph Rowntree Foundation.

Alinsky, S. (1972) *Rules for radicals: A political primer for practical radicals*, New York: Random House.

Allen, A. and May, C. (2007) *Setting up for success: A practical guide for community organisations*, London: Community Development Foundation.

Appiah, K.A. (2007) *The ethics of identity*, Princeton, NJ: Princeton University Press.

Arnstein, S. (1969) 'A ladder of participation in the USA', *Journal of the American Institute of Planners*, 35 (1), 216–40.

Bandura, A. (1994) 'Self-efficacy', in V.S. Ramachaudran (ed) *Encyclopedia of human behavior*, New York: Academic Press, vol 4, pp 71-81.

Banks, S., Butcher, H., Henderson, P. and Robertson, J. (eds) (2013) *Managing community practice: Principles, policies and programmes* (2nd edn), Bristol: Policy Press.

Barr, A. and Hashagen, S. (2000) *ABCD handbook: A framework for evaluating community development*, London: Community Development Foundation.

Batten, T. R. and Batten, M. (1967) *The non-directive approach in group and community work*, Oxford: Oxford University Press.

Baú, V. (2015) 'Building peace through social change communication: Participatory video in conflict-affected communities', *Community Development Journal*, 50(4): 121–37.

Beatty, C. and Fothergill, S. (2013) *Hitting the poorest places hardest: The local and regional impact of welfare reform*, Sheffield: Centre for Regional Economic and Social Research, Sheffield Hallam University.

Beck, D. and Purcell, R. (2010) *Popular education practice for youth and community development work*, Exeter: Learning Matters.

Beck, D. and Purcell, R. (2013) *International community organising*, Bristol: Policy Press.

Beider, H. (2011) *Community cohesion: The views of white working-class communities*, York: Joseph Rowntree Foundation.

Belbin, M. (2009) *The Belbin guide to succeeding at work*, London: A&C Black.

Boal, A. (2008) *Theatre of the oppressed: Get political*, London: Pluto Press.

Bourdieu, P. (1986) 'The forms of capital', in J. Richardson (ed.), *Handbook of theory and research for the sociology of education*, New York: Greenwood Press, pp 241–58.

Bowles, M. (2008) *Democracy: The contribution of community development to local governance and democracy*, London: Community Development Foundation.

BRAP (2015) *From benign neglect to Citizen Khan*, Birmingham: BRAP.

Browne, J. and Levell, P. (2010) *The distributional effect of tax and benefit reforms to be introduced between June 2010 and April 2014: A revised assessment*, London: Institute of Fiscal Studies.

Buchroth, I. and Parkin, C. (2010) *Using theory in youth and community work practice*, Exeter: Learning Matters

Burns, D. (2007) *Systemic action research*, Bristol: The Policy Press.

Burns, D. and Taylor, M. (1998) *Mutual aid and self-help: Coping strategies for excluded communities*, Bristol: The Policy Press.

Burrows, R., Ellison, N. and Woods, B. (2005) *Internet-based neighbourhood information systems and their consequences*, York: Joseph Rowntree Foundation.

Butcher, H., Banks, S., Henderson, P. and Robertson, J. (2007) *Critical community practice*, Bristol: The Policy Press.

Butcher, H., Glen, A., Henderson, P. and Smith, J. (eds) (1993) *Community and public policy*, London: Pluto Press.

Cabinet Office (2010) *Building the Big Society*, www.cabinetoffice.gov.uk/media/407789/building-big-society.pdf

Cabinet Office (2015) *Social action: Harnessing the potential: A discussion paper*, https://www.gov.uk/government/uploads/system/uploads/attachment_data/file/439105/Social_Action_-_Harnessing_the_Potential_updated_June_2015.pdf

Caniglia, B. and Carmin, J. (2005) 'Scholarship on social movement organizations: Classic views and emerging trends', *Mobilization*, 10(2): 201–12.

Capra, F. (1996) *The web of life: A new synthesis of mind and matter*, London: HarperCollins.

Castells, M. (2012) *Networks of outrage and hope: Social movements in the internet age,* Cambridge: Polity Press.

CDFA (now Responsible Finance) (2014) *Inside community finance: The CDFI industry in 2013*, London: Responsible Finance.

CDP (1977) *The costs of industrial change*, London: Community Development Project.

Chambers, R. (1994) *World development*, Amsterdam: Elsevier.

Chang, H-J (2010) *23 things they don't tell you about capitalism*, Harmondsworth: Penguin Books.

Christakis, N. and Fowler, J. (2009). *Connected: The surprising power of our social networks and how they shape our lives*, London: Harper Press.

Clark, T. with Heath, A. (2014) *Hard times: The divisive toll of the economic slump*, New Haven: Yale University Press.

Clegg, S. (1989) *Frameworks of power*, London: Sage Publications.

CLES (Centre for Local Economic Strategies) (2009) *The importance of community anchor organisations to empowerment issues in the North West*, Stockport: North West Together We Can.

CLG (Communities and Local Government) (2006) *The community development challenge*, London: Communities and Local Government.

Coleman, J. (1990) *Foundations of social theory*, Cambridge, MA: Harvard University Press.

Commission on Integration and Cohesion (2007) *Our shared future: Final report of the Commission on Integration and Cohesion*, London: Communities and Local Government.

Commission on Strengthening Local Democracy (2014) *Effective democracy: Reconnecting with communities*, http://www.localdemocracy.info/wp-content/uploads/2014/08/Final-Report-August-2014.pdf

Community Development Exchange (2008) *What is community development?*, Sheffield: CDX, http://www.iacdglobal.org/publications-and-resources/community-development-tools/cdx-resource-what-community-development

Cornwall, A. (2004) 'New democratic spaces? The politics and dynamics of institutionalised participation', *IDS Bulletin*, 35(2): 1–10.

Cox, E. and Schmuecker, K. (2010) *Growing the Big Society: Encouraging success in social and community enterprise in deprived communities*, Newcastle: IPPR (north).

Cox, J., Giorgi, S., Drayson, R. and King, G. (2010) *The Big Green Challenge final evaluation report,* London: Brook Lyndhurst.

Craig, G. (2011) 'Introduction', in G. Craig, M. Mayo, K. Popple, M. Shaw and M. Taylor (eds) *Community development in the United Kingdom 1950–2010*, Bristol: Policy Press, pp 3-21.

Craig, G., Gorman, M. and Vercseg, I. (2004) 'The Budapest Declaration: Building civil society through community development', *Community Development Journal*, 39(4): 423–9.

Craig, G. and Mak, H. W. (2007) *The Hong Kong Declaration: Building democratic institutions and civil society through community development in the Asia-Pacific Region*, Hong Kong: IACD.

Craig, G., Mayo, M., Popple, K., Shaw, M. and Taylor, M. (eds) (2011) *Community development in the United Kingdom 1950–2010*, Bristol: Policy Press.

Craig, G., Mayo, M. and Taylor, M. (1990) 'Empowerment: A continuing role for community development', *Community Development Journal*, 25(4): 286–90.

Craig, G., Popple, K. and Shaw, M. (eds) (2008) *Community development in theory and practice*, Nottingham: Spokesman.

Credit-Suisse (2014) *Global wealth data book, 2014*, Zurich: Credit-Suisse.

Crossley, N. (2002) *Making sense of social movements*, Buckingham: Open University Press.

Crossley, N. (2003) 'From reproduction to transformation: Social movement fields and the radical habitus', *Theory, Culture and Society*, 20(6): 43–68.

Davies, J. (2011) *Challenging governance theory: From networks to hegemony*, Bristol: Policy Press.

Day, G. (2006) *Community and everyday life*, New York: Routledge.

DCLG (2015) *2010 to 2015 government policy: Localism*, https://www.gov.uk/government/publications/2010-to-2015-government-policy-localism/2010-to-2015-government-policy-localism

DeFilippis, J. (2012) 'Community control and development: The long view', in J. DeFilippis and S. Saegert (eds) *The community development reader* (2nd edn), New York: Routledge, pp 30–37.

DeFilippis, J. and Saegert, S. (eds) (2007) *The community development reader*, New York: Routledge.

DeFilippis, J. and Saegert, S. (eds) (2012) *The community development reader* (2nd edn), New York: Routledge.

Defourney, J. and Nyssens, M. (2012) 'Conceptions of social enterprise in Europe: A comparative perspective with the United States', in B. Gidron and Y. Hasenfeld (eds) *Social enterprise: An organizational perspective*, Basingstoke: Palgrave, pp 71–89.

DiMaggio, P. and Powell, W.W. (1983) 'The iron cage revisited: Institutional isomorphism and collective rationality in organizational fields', *American Sociological Review*, 48: 147-60.

Dorling, D. (2015) *Injustice: Why social inequality persists*, Bristol: Policy Press.

Dorsner, C. (2008) 'Implementing the Yaounde Declaration: Practical issues on participatory processes in community development projects', *Community Development Journal*, 43(4): 413–27.

Driver, S. and Martell, L. (1997) 'New Labour's communitarianisms', *Critical Social Policy*, 17(3): 27–46.

Duck, S. (2007) *Human relationships* (4th edn), London: Sage Publications.

Durose, C. and Richardson, L. (2015) *Rethinking public policy-making: Why co-production matters*, Bristol: Policy Press.

Edwards, J. and Batley, R. (1978) *The politics of positive discrimination*, London: Tavistock.

Emejulu, A. (2015) *Community development as micropolitics: Comparing theories, policies and politics in America and Britain*, Bristol: Policy Press.

Equalities Review Team (2007) *Fairness and freedom: The final report of the Equalities Review*, London: CLG.

Etzioni, A. (1998) *The essential communitarian reader*, Lanham, MD: Rowman & Littlefield.

FCDL (Federation for Community Development Learning) (2015) *Community Development National Occupational Standards*, http://www. fcdl.org.uk/learning-qualifications/community-development-national-occupational-standardsFine, B. (2001) *Social capital versus social theory: Political economy and social science at the turn of the millennium*. London: Routledge.

Foot, J. (2010) *A glass half-full: How an asset approach can improve community health and well-being*, London: IDeA.

Foot, J. (2012) *What makes us healthy? The asset based approach in practice: Evidence, action, evaluation*, http://www.scdc.org.uk/media/resources/assets-alliance/What%20makes%20us%20healthy.pdf

Freire, P. (1972) *Pedagogy of the oppressed*, Harmondsworth: Penguin.

Gaventa, J. (2003) *Power after Lukes: A review of the literature*, Brighton: Institute of Development Studies.

GHK (2010) *The national evaluation of community development finance institutions (CDFIs): An action-orientated summary for the sector*, London: Department for Business, Innovation and Skills/Cabinet Office.

Gilchrist, A. (2004) *Community development and community cohesion: Bridges or barricades?*, London: CDF.

Gilchrist, A. (2007) *Equalities and communities: Challenge, choice and change*, London: CDF.

Gilchrist, A. (2009) *The well-connected community: A networking approach to community development* (2nd edn), Bristol: Policy Press.

Gilchrist, A., Wetherell, M. and Bowles, M. (2010) *Social action and identities: Connecting communities for a change*, Basingstoke: Open University Press.

Goetschius, G.W. (1969) *Working with community groups: Using community development as a method of social work*, London: Routledge.

Gramsci, A. (1992) *Prison notebooks (Vol. 1)*, New York: Columbia University Press.

Granovetter, M. (1973) 'The strength of weak ties', *American Journal of Sociology*, 78(6): 1360–80.

Grant-Smith, D. and Matthews, T. (2015) 'Cork as canvas: Exploring intersections of citizenship and collective memory in the Shandon *Big Wash Up* murals', *Community Development Journal*, 50(1): 138–52.

Green, G. and Haines, A. (2015) *Asset building and community development*, London: Sage Publications.

Habermas, J. (1984) *The theory of communicative action: Vol. 1: Reason and the rationalisation of society*, Cambridge: Polity Press.

Halpern, D. (2005) *Social capital*, Cambridge: Polity Press.

Halpern, D. (2009) *The hidden wealth of nations*, Cambridge: Polity Press.

Halpern, D. (2015) *Inside the Nudge Unit: How small changes can make a big difference*, London: WH Allen.

Harris, V. (ed.) (2009) *Community work skills manual 2009*, Sheffield: Federation for Community Development Learning.

Hawtin, M. and Percy-Smith, J. (2007) *Community profiling: A practical guide* (2nd edn), Buckingham: Open University Press.

Henderson, P. and Thomas, D. (2013) *Skills in neighbourhood work* (4th edn), Abingdon: Routledge.

Henderson, P. and Vercseg, I. (2010) *Community development and civil society: Making connections in the European context*, Bristol: Policy Press.

Hillery, G. (1955) 'Definitions of community: Areas of agreement', *Rural Sociology*, 20: 111–23.

Hills, J. (2010) *An anatomy of economic inequality in the UK: Report of the National Equality Panel*, London: Government Equalities Office.

Hofstede, G. (2001) *Culture's consequences: Comparing values, behaviors, institutions and organizations across nations* (2nd edn). Thousand Oaks, CA: Sage Publications.

Hoggett, P., Mayo, M. and Miller, C. (2009) *The dilemmas of development work: Ethical challenges in regeneration*, Bristol: Policy Press.

Hope, A. and Timmel, S. (2013) *Training for transformation in practice*, Rugby: Practical Action Publishing.

Howard, J. and Taylor, M. (2010) 'Hybridity in partnerships: Managing tensions and opportunities', in D. Billis (ed.) *The erosion of the third sector? Hybrid organisations in a new welfare landscape*, Basingstoke: Palgrave Macmillan, pp 175-96.

IACD (2015a) *Annual review 2014/15*, http://www.iacdglobal.org/publications-and-resources/annual-reviews

IACD (2015b) *Mapping of community development training and education programs and national CD practitioner support organizations and networks*, http://www.iacdglobal.org/files/iacd_report_on_mapping_project_2015.pdf

Ife, J. (2013) *Community development in an uncertain world: Vision, analysis and practice*, Melbourne: Cambridge University Press.

Ife, J. and Tesoriero, F. (2006) *Community development: Community-based alternatives in an age of globalisation* (3rd edn), Sydney: Pearson Australia.

Imagine (2015) *Community Organisers Programme legacy report*, London: Locality.

Independence Panel (2015) *An independent mission: The voluntary sector in 2015*, London: The Baring Foundation.

Ishkanian, A. and Szreter, S. (2012) *The Big Society debate: A new agenda for social welfare?* Cheltenham: Edward Elgar.

Jackson, A. and O'Doherty, C. (2012) *Community development in Ireland: Theory, policy & practice*, Dublin: Gill and Macmillan.

Kahneman, D. and Tversky, A. (eds) (2000) *Choices, values and frames*, New York: Cambridge University Press.

Keen, R. (2015) *Membership of UK political parties*, Briefing paper SN05125, London: House of Commons Library.

Kenny , S., Taylor, M., Onyx, J. and Mayo, M. (2015) *Challenging the third sector: Global prospects for active citizenship*, Bristol: Policy Press.

Kim, S. (2016) 'Silent counteractions of community organizations in a welfare partnership: a case study of South Korean workfare agencies', *Community Development Journal*, 51(1).

Knapp, M., Bauer, M., Perkins, M and Snell, T. (2013) 'Building community capital in social care: Is there an economic case?', *Community Development Journal*, 48(2): 313–31.

Kolb, D.A. (1984) *Experiential Learning*, Englewood Cliffs, NJ: Prentice Hall.

Kretzmann, J. and McKnight, J. (1993) *Building communities from the inside out: A path toward finding and mobilizing a community's assets*, Evanston, IL: Institute for Policy Research, Northwestern University.

Kretzmann, J. and McKnight, J. (2003) 'Introduction to asset mapping', www.abcdinstitute.org/docs/abcd/IntroAssetMapping.pdf

Ledwith, M. (1997) *Participating in transformation: Towards a working model of community empowerment*, Birmingham: Venture Press.

Ledwith, M. (2011) *Community development: A critical approach* (2nd edn), Bristol: Policy Press.

Ledwith, M. (2015) *Community development in action: Putting Freire into practice*, Bristol: Policy Press.

Ledwith, M. and Springett, J. (2010) *Participatory practice: Community based action for transformative change*, Bristol: Policy Press.

Lesniewski, J. and Canon, R. (2016) 'Worker centers, cities and grassroots regulation of the labour market', *Community Development Journal*, 51(1).

LEWRG (London Edinburgh Weekend Return Group) (1979) *In and against the state*, London: Pluto Press.

Lipsky, M. (1980) *Street-level bureaucracy: Dilemmas of the individual in public services*, New York: Russell Sage Foundation.

Loney, M. (1983) *Community against government*, London: Heinemann.

Longstaff, B. (2008) *The community development challenge: Evaluation: Establishing an outcomes and evidence base*, London: Community Development Foundation.

Lukes, S. (2005) *Power: A radical view* (2nd edn), Basingstoke: Palgrave Macmillan.

Marmot, M. (2010) *Fair society, healthy lives*, London: UCL.

Marmot, M. (2015) *The health gap: The challenge of an unequal world*, London: Bloomsbury.

Marris, P. and Rein, M. (1967) *Dilemmas of social reform*, New York: Atherton Press.

Maslow, A. (1943) 'A theory of human motivation', *Psychological Review*, 50(4): 370–96.

Mathie, A. and Cunningham, G. (eds) (2008) *From clients to citizens: Communities changing the course of their own development*, Rugby: Practical Action.

Mayo, M. (1975) 'Community development: A radical alternative', in R. Bailey and M. Brake (eds) *Radical social work*, London: Arnold, pp 129-43.

Mayo, M. and Annette, J. (eds) (2010) *Taking part? Active learning for active citizenship and beyond?*, Leicester: NIACE Publications.

Mayo, M., Mendiwelso-Bendek, Z. and Packham, C. (2013) *Community research for community development*, Basingstoke: Palgrave Macmillan.

McAdam, D., McCarthy, J. and Zald, M. (1996) *Comparative perspectives on social movements*, Cambridge: Cambridge University Press.

McCabe, A., Phillimore, P. and Mayblin, L. (2010) *'Below the radar' activities and organisations in the third sector: A summary review of the literature*, TSRC Working Paper 29, Birmingham: Third Sector Research Centre.

McCabe, A., Gilchrist, A., Afridi, A., Harris, K. and Kyprianou, P. (2013) *Making the links: Poverty, ethnicity and social networks*, York: Joseph Rowntree Foundation.

McMorland, J. and Erakovic, L. (2013) *Stepping through transitions: Management, leadership and governance in non-for-profit organisations*, Auckland, New Zealand: CGO Transitions Limited.

Melucci, A. (1988) 'Social movements and the democratisation of everyday life', in J. Keane (ed.) *Civil society and the state*, London: Verso, pp 245–60.

Melucci, A. (1996) *Challenging codes: Collective action in the information age*, Cambridge: Cambridge University Press.

Miller, C. (2008) *The community development challenge: Management*, London: Community Development Foundation.

Miller, P. and Rose, N. (2009) *Governing the present*, Cambridge: Polity Press.

Morris, J., Cobbing, P., Leach, K. and Conaty, P. (2013) *Mainstreaming community economic development*, Birmingham: Localise West Midlands.

Mundle, C., Naylor, C. and Buck, D. (2012) *Volunteering in health and care in England: A summary of key literature*, London: The King's Fund.

Murtagh, B. and Goggin, N. (2015) 'Finance, social economics and community development', *Community Development Journal*, 50(3): 494–509.

National Coalition for Independent Action (2015) *Fight or flight: The voluntary sector in 2015*, London: NCIA.

National Institute for Health and Clinical Excellence (2008) *Community engagement to improve health*, London: NICE.

NCVO (National Council for Voluntary Organisations) (2015) *A financial sustainability review of the voluntary sector*, London: NCVO.

New Economics Foundation (2010) *Catalysts for community action and investment: A social return on investment analysis of community development work based on a common outcomes framework*. London: NEF/CDF.

Nisbet, R. (1953) *The quest for community*, Oxford: Oxford University Press.

Noya, A., Clarence, E. and Craig, G. (eds) (2009) *Community capacity building: Creating a better future together*, Paris: OECD Publishing.

Ockenden, N. and Hutin, M. (2008) *Volunteering to lead: A study of leadership within small volunteer-led groups*. London: IVR.

O'Connor, A. (2012) 'Swimming against the tide: A brief history of federal policy to poorer communities', in J. DeFilippis and S. Saegert (eds) *The community development reader*, New York: Routledge, pp 11–29.

O'Mara-Eves, A., Brunton G., McDaid, D., Oliver, S., Kavanagh, J, Jamal, F. et al (2013) 'Community engagement to reduce inequalities in health: A systematic review, meta-analysis and economic analysis', *Public Health Research* 1(4).

Orme, J., Powell, J., Taylor, P. and Grey, M. (eds) *Public health for the 21st century: New perspectives on policy, participation and practice* (2nd edn), Maidenhead: McGraw-Hill Education/Open University Press.

Packham, C (2000) 'Community auditing and community development', in B. Humphries (ed.), *Applied social research: A reader,* Manchester: MMU Publications.

Packham, C. (2008) *Active citizenship and community learning*, Exeter: Learning Matters.

Parsfield, M., Morris, D., Bola, M., Knapp, M., Yoshioka, M. and Marcus, G. (2015) *Community capital: The value of connected communities*, London: RSA.

Pearce, J., Howard, J. and Bronstein, A. (2010) 'Editorial: Learning from Latin America', *Community Development Journal*, 45(3): 265–76.

Pestoff, V. and Brandsen, T. (eds) (2008) *Co-production, the third sector and the delivery of public services*, London and New York: Routledge.

Pestoff, V., Brandsen, T. and Verschuere, B. (eds) (2012) *New public governance, the third sector & co-production*, London and New York: Routledge.

Piketty, T. (2013) *Capital in the twenty-first century*, London: Belknap Press.

Pitchford, M. and Henderson, P. (2008) *Making spaces for community development*, Bristol, The Policy Press.

Plant, R. (1974) *Community and ideology: An essay in applied social philosophy*, London: Routledge & Kegan Paul.

Popple, K. (2015) *Analysing community work: Its theory and practice* (2nd edn), Buckingham: Open University Press.

Portes, A. (1995) 'Economic sociology and the sociology of immigration: A conceptual overview', in A. Portes (ed) *The economic sociology of immigration*, New York: Russell Sage Foundation, pp 1-41.

Purkis, A. (2012) 'Big Society contractors? Big questions for voluntary organisations', *Voluntary Sector Review*, 3(1): 93-101.

Putnam, R. (1993) *Making democracy work*, Princeton, NJ: Princeton University Press.

Rabinow, P. (ed) (1984) *The Foucault reader*, London: Penguin.

Richardson, L. (2008) *DIY community action: Neighbourhood problems and community self-help*, Bristol: The Policy Press.

Rochester, C. (1999) *Juggling on a unicycle: A handbook for small voluntary agencies*, London: Centre for Voluntary Organisations, London School of Economics and Political Science.

Rochester, C. (2013) *Rediscovering voluntary action*. Basingstoke: Palgrave Macmillan.

Rose, N. (1999) *Powers of freedom: Reframing political thought*, Cambridge: Cambridge University Press.

Rose, N. and Miller, P. (1992) 'Political power beyond the state: Problematics of government', *British Journal of Sociology*, 43(2): 173–205.

Rothman, J. with Tropman, J. (1970) 'Models of community organization and macro practice perspectives: their mixing and phasing', in F. Cox, J. Erlich, J. Rothman and J. Tropman (eds) *Strategies of community organization*, (4th edn) Itasca, Il: F. E. Peacock Publishers, pp 3-25.

Russell, C. (2015) *Asset based community development (ABCD): Looking back to look forward: In conversation with John McKnight about the intellectual and practical heritage of ABCD and its place in the world today* [e-book] Available to download from https://itunes.apple.com/GB/book/id1007493751?l=en

Ryder, A., Cemlyn, S. and Acton, T. (2014) *Hearing the voices of Gypsy, Roma and Traveller communities*, Bristol: Policy Press.

Sabatier, P. (1988) 'An advocacy coalition framework of policy change and the role of policy-oriented learning therein', *Policy Sciences*, 21: 129–68.

Sampson, R. (2004) 'Neighbourhood and community: Collective efficacy and community safety', *New Economy*, 11: 106–13.

Sampson, R. (2012), 'What community supplies', in J. DeFilippis and S. Saegert (eds) *The community development reader*, New York: Routledge, pp 308 –18.

Sampson, R., Morenoff, J. and Gannon-Rowley, T. (2002) 'Assessing neighbourhood effects: Social processes and new directions in research', *Annual Review of Sociology*, 28: 443–78.

Sen, A. (2009) *The idea of justice*, London: Allen Lane.

Sender, H., Carlisle, B., Hatamian, A. and Bowles, M. (2010) *Report on survey of community development practitioners and managers*, London: Community Development Foundation.

Seyfang, G. (2009) *The new economics of sustainable consumption: Seeds of change*, Basingstoke: Palgrave.

Shaw, M. (2004) *Community work: Policy, politics and practice*, Hull: Universities of Hull and Edinburgh.

Shaw, M., Meagher, J. and Moir, S. (2006) *Participation in community development: Problems and possibilities*, Edinburgh: Concept with the *Community Development Journal*.

Sherraden, M. and Ninacs, W. (eds) (2014) *Community economic development and social work*, New York: Routledge.

Sievers, S. (2016) 'Fragile heterotopias – a case study of a Danish social enterprise', *Community Development Journal*, 51(1).

Skinner, S. and Farrar, G. (2009) *Liberating leadership: A fresh perspective*, London: Community Sector Coalition.

Skinner, S. and Wilson, M. (2008) *Assessing community strengths*, London: Community Development Foundation.

Smock, K. (2004) *Democracy in action: Community organizing and urban change*, New York: Columbia University Press.

Somerville, P. (2011) *Understanding community: Politics, policy and practice*, Bristol: The Policy Press.

South, J., Stansfield, J. and Mehta, P. (2015) *A guide to community centred approaches for health and well-being*, London: Public Health England.

Stoker, G. (1998) 'Governance as theory: five propositions', *International Social Science Journal*, 50(155): 17–28.

Stuteley, H. and Parish, R. (2010) *The emergence of the H.E.L.P. practice model: from apathy to anger to positive energy*, London: Health Empowerment Leverage Project.

Swanepoel, H. and De Beer, F. (2012) *Community development: Breaking the cycle of poverty* (5th edn), Claremont, South Africa: Juta Academic.

Tarrow, S. (2011) *Power in movement: Social movements and contentious politics*, Cambridge: Cambridge University Press.

Taylor, M. (2011) *Public policy in the community* (2nd edn), Basingstoke: Palgrave Macmillan.

Taylor, M. (2012) 'The changing fortunes of community', *Voluntary Sector Review*, 3(1): 15–34.

Taylor, M. and Wilson, M. (2015) *Changing communities: Supporting voluntary and community organisations to adapt to local demographic and cultural change*, London: The Baring Foundation.

Taylor, M. and Wilson, M. (2016, forthcoming) 'Community organising for social change: The scope for class politics', in M. Shaw and M. Mayo (eds) *Class, inequality and community development*, Bristol: Policy Press.

Taylor, M., Wilson, M., Purdue, D. and Wilde, P. (2007) *Changing neighbourhoods: Lessons from the JRF Neighbourhood Programme*, York: Joseph Rowntree Foundation.

Thaler, R. and Sunstein, C. (2008) *Improving decisions about health, wealth, and happiness*, New Haven, CT: Yale University Press.

Thornham, H. and Parry, K. (2015) 'Constructing communities: The community centre as contested site', *Community Development Journal*, 50(1): 24–39.

Trenberth, K., Fasullo, J. and Shepherd, T. (2015) 'Attribution of climate extreme events', *Nature Climate Change*, 5, 725–30.

Tuckman, B.W. (1965) 'Developmental sequence in small groups', *Psychological Bulletin*, 63(6): 384–99.

Twelvetrees, A. (forthcoming) *Community work* (5th edn), Basingstoke: Palgrave Macmillan.

United Nations (1955) *Social progress through community development*, New York: United Nations.

Walker, G.P., Hunter, S., Devine-Wright, P., Evans, B. and Fay, H. (2007) 'Harnessing community energies: Explaining and evaluating community-based localism in renewable energy policy in the UK', *Global Environmental Politics*, 7(2): 64–82.

Warhurst, P. and Dobson, J. (2014) *Incredible! Plant veg and grow a revolution*, Kibworth Beauchamp: Matador.

Wellman, B. (1979) 'The community question: the intimate networks of East Yorkers', *American Journal of Sociology*, 84(5): 1201–31.

Wetherell, M. (ed) (2009) *Theorizing identities and social action*, Basingstoke: Palgrave.

Whitney, D. and Trosten-Bloom, A. (2010) *The power of appreciative Inquiry* (2nd edn), San Francisco, CA: Berrett-Koehler.

Wilkinson, R. and Pickett, K (2009) *The spirit level: Why equality is better for everyone*, London: Penguin.

Wind-Cowie, M. (2010) *Civic streets: The Big Society in action*, London: Demos.

Woodin, T., Crook, D. and Carpentier, V. (2010) *Community and mutual ownership: A historical review*, York: Joseph Rowntree Foundation.

Woolcock, M. (1998) 'Social capital and economic development: Toward a theoretical synthesis and policy framework', *Theory and Society*, 27(2): 151–208.

World Commission on Environment and Development (1987) *Our common future: Report of the World Commission on Environment and Development* (The Brundtland Report), Oxford: Oxford University Press.

Young, M. and Willmott, P. (1957) *Family and kinship in East London*, London: Institute of Community Studies.

appendix: resources

The main community development organisations in the UK

ACORN

ACORN started as a movement of community organisers in the US and has grown to a national organisation with a series of branches in the UK. It supports its members to improve neighbourhoods; influence employers, landlords, businesses and authorities; run projects and services to help each other; and fight for economic and social change.

CWU, 20 Church Rd, Lawrence Hill, Bristol BS5 9JA
No phone number
www.acorncommunities.org.uk

Action with Communities in Rural England (ACRE)

ACRE promotes the interests of rural communities. It also acts as the national umbrella organisation for 38 Rural Community Councils throughout England. ACRE aims to promote a healthy, vibrant and sustainable rural community sector that is well connected to policies and initiatives at national, regional, sub-regional and local levels. ACRE's organisational vision is to provide a rural community development centre of expertise that is extensively used by policy makers and practitioners.

Suite 109, Unit 9, Cirencester Office Park, Tetbury Road, Cirencester, Gloucestershire GL7 6JJ
Telephone: 01285 653477
www.acre.org.uk

Citizens UK

Citizens UK organises communities to act together for power, social justice and the common good. It describes itself as the home of community organising in the UK, with diverse civil society alliances in London, Milton Keynes, Nottingham, Birmingham, Wales and Leeds. Its main focus is developing the leadership capacity of its members so they can hold politicians and other decision-makers to account on the issues that matter to them.

112 Cavell Street, London E1 2JA
Telephone: 020 7043 9881
www.citizensuk.org

Company of Community Organisers (COLtd)

COLtd is the legacy body of the government-funded Community Organisers programme. It is a member-led training and support organisation that encourages social action in neighbourhoods across England.

The Elsie Whiteley Innovation Centre, Hopwood Lane, Halifax HX1 5ER
Email: admin@corganisers.org.uk
Telephone: 01985 217048
www.corganisers.org.uk

Community Development Cymru (CDC)

Community Development Cymru (CDC) is a national community development organisation for Wales. CDC's mission is to improve the quality of life for the poorest and most disadvantaged communities in Wales by challenging inequality, discrimination and social injustice. CDC is a membership organisation and the voice of community development in Wales.

Plas Dolerw, Milford Road, Newtown, Powys SY16 2EH
Telephone: 01686 627377
www.cdcymru.org

Community Links

Community Links is an innovative East London charity, running a wide range of community projects for over 16,000 people every year. Based in Newham, they have over 30 years of experience working with local people to support children, young people, adults and families. Through its national work, lessons are shared with government and community groups across the country to achieve social change.

105 Barking Road, Canning Town, London E16 4HQ
Telephone: 020 7473 2270
www.community-links.org

Community Matters

Community Matters is the national membership and support organisation for the community sector. It champions voluntary and community action at neighbourhood level as a means of local people taking control of issues in their area and fostering community spirit.

12–20 Baron Street, London N1 9LL
Telephone: 020 7837 7887
www.communitymatters.org.uk

Community Workers' Co-operative (CWC)

Established in 1981, the Community Workers' Co-operative (CWC) is a national organisation that promotes and supports community work in Ireland as a means of addressing poverty, social exclusion and inequality, and ultimately as a means of achieving social change that will contribute to the creation of a more just, sustainable and equal society. The CWC is a membership organisation and currently has approximately 800 individual and organisational members.

CWC National Office, c/o Galway Traveller Movement, 1 The Plaza, Headford Road, Galway
Telephone: +353 (0) 74 912 8792
www.cwc.ie

Federation for Community Development Learning (FCDL)

FCDL supports community development through advancing and promoting good quality community development learning and practice at local, regional and national (UK-wide) levels. FCDL works to provide a network to support the development, evaluation and dissemination of good quality community development learning, training and qualification opportunities.

8 Paradise Street, Sheffield S1 2DF
Tel: 0114 258 7270
www.fcdl.org.uk

Federation of City Farms and Community Gardens (FCFCG)

FCFCG works with community farms and gardens, school farms, care farms, wildlife and roof gardens, community orchards, community-run allotments and community-supported agriculture schemes. Its aim is to help grass roots groups create genuine benefits for their community.

The Green House, Hereford Street, Bristol BS3 4NA
Telephone: 0117 923 1800
www.farmgarden.org.uk

Locality

Locality is the national network formed from the merger of Bassac (the British Association of Settlements and Social Action Centres) and the Development Trusts Association. It works with members on community asset ownership, collaboration, commissioning support, social enterprise, community voice and advocacy.

33 Corsham Street, London N1 6DR
Tel: 0345 458 8336
www.locality.org.uk

Local Trust
Local Trust supports communities through managing a large-scale funding programme (currently Big Local). Its mission is to enable residents to make their communities and their areas even better places in which to live. By providing a mixture of funding and finance, it helps them to develop and use their skills and confidence to identify what matters most to them, and to take action to change things for the better, now and in the future.

Unit D, 15-18 White Lion Street, London N1 9PD
Tel: 020 3588 0565
www.localtrust.org.uk

National Association for Voluntary and Community Action (NAVCA)
NAVCA is the national voice of *local support and development organisations* in England. It champions and strengthens voluntary and community action by supporting its members in their work with over 160,000 local charities and community groups

The Tower, 2 Furnival Square, Sheffield S1 4QL
Tel: 0114 278 6636
www.navca.org.uk

Scottish Community Development Centre (SCDC)
SCDC supports best practice in community development and is recognised by the Scottish Government as the national lead body for community development. It works across sectors and with a wide range of professions to support community engagement and community capacity building in any context and at strategic and practice level.

Suite 305, Baltic Chambers, 50 Wellington Street, Glasgow G2 6HJ
Telephone: 0141 248 1924
www.scdc.org.uk

Scottish Community Development Network (SCDN)

SCDN is a member-led organisation, for community workers/community development workers, paid or unpaid, full-or part-time, from the community, voluntary or public sectors, who support the principles and practice of community development. SCDN is open to anyone with an interest in community development in Scotland.

PO Box 26792, Glasgow G4 7AF.
No telephone
www.scdn.org.uk

Voice4Change (England)

The national membership organisation championing the voice of the BME voluntary, community and social enterprise sector in policy making. It aims to make a long-term positive difference to BME and other disadvantaged communities, by speaking to policy makers to drive more informed and responsive policy making, and support civil society organisations that emerge from and work with these communities to provide support and drive social change.

Studio 21, 1 Filament Walk, Wandsworth, London SW18 4GQ
Tel: 020 3405 5210
www.voice4change-england.co.uk

International community development organisations

Community Development Society International (CDSI)

CDSI is US-based but has members throughout the world. It organises international conferences and publishes a journal.

www.comm-dev.org

International Association for Community Development (IACD)
IACD is the only global network for professional community development practitioners. It supports development agencies and practitioners to build the capacity of communities, to realise greater social and economic equality, environmental protection and political democracy. It is a non-governmental organisation accredited with the UN.

The Stables, Falkland, Fife KY15 7AF
Tel: +44 (0)131 618 8394
www.iacdglobal.org

The European Community Development Network (EuCDN)
EuCDN brings together a variety of partners from countries in and outside the EU to promote community development and facilitate exchanges, learning and joint projects between members.

www.eucdn.net

Opportunities for further study and training

There are a number of courses in the UK that support learning on community development, some of which lead to a professional qualification. The courses in youth and community (which are mostly at degree level) can be found through the website of the National Youth Agency (www.nya.org.uk).

In addition, there are a number of short courses, including one-day workshops, which provide taster sessions or very specific skills-based learning. You can find out about these from the websites of organisations such as the Federation for Community Development Learning, the National Association for Voluntary and Community Action, Tenants Participation Advisory Service (www@tpas.org.uk) and others listed in this appendix.

Index

Note: 'CD' refers to 'community development'